Vision Impact!

How to Realize Your Vision, Implement Your Plan and Impact Your World

Bernard K. Haynes

Vision Impact! How to Realize Your Vision, Implement Your Plan and Impact Your World
by Bernard K. Haynes
Copyright © 2013 Lead to Impact™, LLC

For more materials and information contact:

Bernard K. Haynes
Lead to Impact, LLC
bhaynes@leadtoimpact.com
www.leadtoimpact.com

ISBN:9780996194549
For Worldwide Distribution
Printed in the U.S.A

Published by:
Lead to Impact LLC
3740 Falls Tr.
Winston, GA 30187

ACKNOWLEDGMENTS

To my loving and beautiful wife Dana, who has been with me through thick and thin: You supported me during the process of writing this book and listened to me talk about it for three years. You encouraged me to keep moving forward when I doubted I could do it. I will always love you.

To Jordan and Jalen, my two wonderful boys: Thank you for sharing me during this project. I know God has an incredible vision for your lives. I love you, but most of all God loves you more.

Most importantly, I thank God for giving me the vision and using me as a vessel to deliver this message of inspiration, truth and personal transformation.

CONTENTS

~ INTRODUCTION ~

"No individual has any right to come into the world and go out of it without leaving behind him distinct and legitimate reasons for having passed through it."
—George Washington Carver

You were born with the potential to live an extraordinary life. Your journey to extraordinary living includes realizing who you are and why you are here. When you discover the answers to these questions, your life will change. You will become more energized and excited to live each day. You will begin to think, talk and walk with a different motivation. You will no longer allow yesterday's failures and today's circumstances to keep you from moving toward tomorrow's promises. You will not focus on the negativity and pessimism from others, but you will live life moving forward.

Vision Impact! *How to Realize Your Vision, Implement Your Plan and Impact Your World*, contains forty-two short, easy-to-read inspiring messages that present practical insight, instruction and inspiration on how to develop and implement your personal and/or family vision plan. If you are serious about living your vision, you can develop and implement a vision plan within forty-two days (six weeks) that will take your life to a new dimension.

Each message is like a vision energy drink to encourage, equip and empower you to take action on living out your vision. These are not magical formulas you read so that suddenly everything in your life works as planned. Each message was written to help you succeed through your vision process.

You do not have to read these messages in any particular order. You can open the book and begin with any message. You may see some points covered more than once, but this adds emphasis and solidifies the vision message more powerfully in your thoughts, speech and actions.

Now is the time for you to awaken the vision that lives inside of you. It is time for you to create a vision plan that gives your life and family direction. I am talking about a written vision plan that focuses on every area of your life. Your written vision plan helps you to see where you are going, what changes you need to make and if you are progressing toward your designed future.

You cannot afford to spend the next year, or the next five, ten or twenty years, talking and thinking about what should've, could've or would've been.

Get Ready. Get Set. Realize Your Vision. Implement Your Plan. And Impact Your World.

CHAPTER 1

VISION IMPACT!

"Where there is no vision the people perish...."
—Proverbs 29:18

Do you have a clearly written vision that impacts your life and family? What is vision? Vision is a clear mental picture of a preferable future that God communicates to an individual. The individual becomes so committed to the vision that he or she will pursue it despite any obstacles or challenges. It is the ingredient that launches an individual out of stagnation and into forward action.

Visions originate in the heart and mind of someone who is frustrated and tired of the way things are in contrast to the way he believes things could and should be.

It was the vision of equal rights for all people that inspired Dr. Martin Luther King, Jr. to crusade for civil rights. It was the vision of a new nation of people that led Abraham to leave his homeland to follow God to an unfamiliar land. It was the vision of greater discovery that motivated George Washington Carver to discover over 300 different uses for the peanut. It was the vision of becoming a fisher of men that led Peter to leave his fishing business to follow Jesus. Vision demands change.

What is possibly more satisfying than knowing the God of the universe designed you with a unique vision to impact the world? His vision for you is not a one-size-fits-all, but it is uniquely fashioned to fit you. No matter who you are, what country or continent you live on or what side of the tracks you are from, God created you with a specific vision that no one in this world can live but you.

I do not care who tries to imitate your vision; he will never live it as effectively as you. Even if he follows it step-by-step and word-for-word, he will never execute it the way you can. The tragedy is to live your entire life without ever living to the full potential of your unique vision.

One of the major dilemmas in today's contemporary, fast-paced, over-communicated society is the number of people living without ever realizing their unique vision. Knowledge and communication are just one click away. Instant gratification is an obsession. Patience is a lost virtue. If we cannot have what we want when we want it, we oftentimes find ourselves disappointed, distressed and discouraged.

Many people are busy moving at fast-break speeds hourly, daily, weekly, monthly and yearly, but they still have no real vision beyond their current situations. They spend countless hours talking and texting on mobile devices, watching their favorite reality shows or emailing, tweeting and checking their Facebook pages, but many fail to spend the same quality time seeking God for their life's direction.

Thus, they live void of the unique vision that can catapult them to extraordinary living. A lack of vision causes many to miss the great and settle for what they think is good. God uniquely created you to live an exceptional life.

Our world is in desperate need of individuals who possess a clear vision from God: a vision that comes from Him and belongs to you personally, and not a vision dictated by contemporary society, traditional religion or someone else's image.

God provides you the necessary tools to live effectively: the presence of His Holy Spirit, His Word, spiritual and natural gifts and a desire to succeed. These tools will inspire a hunger and passion in you to relentlessly pursue your vision like never before.

Regardless of where you are in life, (your age, financial status, educational level or family background) your unique vision positions you to impact your home, community, city, state, nation and ultimately the world! The desire to impact those connected to your vision empowers you to move past the failures of yesterday, the excuses of today and the fears of tomorrow.

When you take the initiative to activate your vision, it will:

- Give you the correct directions and coordinates to follow.

- Let you know where you currently are and what turns you need to make to get to your destination.

- Provide the inspiration and motivation you need when it seems everything and everyone is against you.

- Expand your thinking, increase your sight and elevate your walk.

Get ready to take hold of your vision and impact your world!

"The most pathetic person in the world is someone who has sight, but has no vision."
— Helen Keller

CHAPTER 2

GET OFF YOUR I-285

"The Lord our God spoke to us at Horeb saying, you have stayed long enough at this mountain. Turn and take your journey…"
— *Deuteronomy 1:6-7*

Several years ago, my wife and I were traveling on I-285 in Atlanta going to a shopping center. To those who may not know, I-285 is the by-pass loop that goes around the perimeter of Atlanta. What should have been a forty-five minute trip took us an hour and a half.

I will never forget riding around I-285. I said to my wife, "I believe we have passed the airport twice." She looked at me with frustration in her eyes, anger in her voice, and said, "No, this is our third time." I knew then it was time to ask for proper directions. I let go of my I-know-where–I-am-going ego and asked for directions. It didn't make sense to continue riding around in circles when help was a phone call away.

I believe to this day one of two things occurred: I received bad directions or I didn't write the directions down correctly. My wife says that I did not listen. In any case, we wasted valuable time and gas riding around the perimeter of Atlanta.

The children of Israel experienced the first I-285 experience. It took forty years for them to complete a less than two-week journey. They spent forty years wandering in circles instead of enjoying the prosperous land God promised them. They exhausted valuable time and energy going around and around the same mountain, passing through the same desert land because they refused to obey God's directions.

The children of Israel forfeited forty years of abundant living in the land flowing with milk and honey because they allowed fear, rebellion and disobedience to block their promise. It wasn't the distance to the land that stood in their way of receiving the promise; it was the attitude of their hearts.

I learned from my I-285 experiences that time waits for no one. You can choose to keep going around in circles because you fear change, you are intimidated about what someone might do or say, or you are scared of losing some material things or relationships. I discovered you can lose a lot more if you continue going around the perimeter of your life.

If you lose some material things, you can work to get them back. If you lose a job, you can eventually get another job. If you lose your house, you can find another place to live. If your good credit is lost, over time you can build your credit back. But the major thing I learned from my I-285 experiences is you cannot get the time back you lose going in circles. Once the time is gone, it is gone. No matter how much you want to turn back the hands of time, you cannot.

It is crazy to continue to go around the same circles when help is a prayer away. God gives clear directions to where He wants you to go. You cannot move forward traveling around in circles. If you do, you will live your life in insanity. And one definition of insanity is to do the same thing over and over again expecting a different result.

Now is the time for you to reach your destination. It is time to end the insanity. It is time to change direction and get new results. It is time to enjoy what's inside the perimeter of your life.

Today is your day to get off your I-285 and experience all life has to offer. The journey is not easy, but you can make it. You will encounter frustration and fatigue when you can't seem to find the correct exit ramp.

You can overcome frustration and fatigue if you:

- Stop trying to find your own way.
- Stop following your wrong directions.
- Stop listening to people's opinions on what you need to do and where you need to go.
- Stop conforming to the status quo.

Just as I made a phone call to get the right directions to exit off I-285 toward my destination, you must make the decision to seek God for the right directions to get off your personal I-285. When you do, you will arrive at your designed destination in excellent time.

> *"We are what we repeatedly do. Excellence, therefore, is not an act but a habit."*
> *— Aristotle*

CHAPTER 3

WHY VISION MATTERS

"For we are His workmanship, created in Christ Jesus for good works, which God prepared beforehand so that we would walk in them."
— Ephesians 2:10

Vision matters because it generates hope in the midst of despair and provides comfort when things are chaotic. It empowers you to overcome the limitations of what the eyes see as impossible. It opens your mind and heart to what faith knows is possible. Vision matters because God says it matters.

1. Vision energizes purpose.
God created you with an original purpose in mind. The fact that you are alive today, the reason you have gone through everything you have gone through and the reason the enemy could not take you out, is evidence God has a greater purpose for your life.

You must fight through everything and everyone who tries to keep you from living your vision. The enemy's strategy is to keep you in the dark about your true purpose. He wants you to focus on your past instead of looking to your promised future. He wants you to live life discouraged and defeated instead of encouraged and empowered. A vision from God will energize you to live above the enemy's attacks.

2. Vision enlivens confidence.
I want to go back to Ephesians 2:10, where you are called His workmanship. I want you to say out loud, "I am God's workmanship." Say it like you believe it! Say it with authority! Say it with absolute confidence even if you don't feel it!

Can you comprehend what you just declared in the atmosphere? Do you understand what this means? It means you possess unwavering confidence that God designed you specifically to accomplish His vision for your life. He has determined who you should become. He has paved the road to your destiny. It is up to you whether you stay where you are or begin to move in confidence toward your unique vision.

3. Vision empowers success.

The most common problem I find today when talking to people is the lack of a clearly defined vision that gives them direction. When asked what success would look like for them, many find it difficult to answer with specific details. I challenge them with these questions:

How can you live successfully if you don't know God's vision for your life? Can you describe your vision in vivid detail, as it would look in complete success? If not, you have work to do. You must spend some quality time seeking God in prayer and mediating on His Word to realize your vision and how to live it successfully.

Over the course of time, you should be able to clearly articulate your life's purpose and vision. The problem with not being able to do so is you will have no real direction in which to aim your efforts. Zig Ziglar says it this way: "If you aim at nothing, you will hit it every time."

4. Vision exposes opportunities.

Opportunities aren't stumbled upon, they are created! God created them for you before you were ever born. Your opportunities for success await your full participation. So go out and put your vision into action and watch the new opportunities spring up.

Meet new people, take a class on a new subject, visit a new place, write out your business plan, plan a vision retreat, update your resume and send it out then follow-up with the people you sent it to.

In other words, live life on purpose! Don't wait for your big break; live your own big break. Don't wait for the right company to hire you; create your own company. Don't sit back and wait for others to approve your vision; start living it today. Define what vision success means for you and then chart a path to reach that success. You will be glad you did!

5. Vision encourages forward movement.

God designed you with a vision to propel you forward in living a successful life. I call it Vision Impact Living, meaning you are intentionally living your unique vision in every area of life and it makes a lasting impact in your world.

Allow God to direct your life. Trust Him to steer the ship. You can no longer blame your family, friends, the government, your job, where you were born, or the economy for where you are in life. It is up to you to do what you need to do to position yourself for vision success.

Understand that your vision grows and changes over time. What is right for you now may develop into something different in a few years. Being clear on what is deeply important to you and pursuing it passionately helps you grow and develop into the person God destined you to be. As you tirelessly work on becoming a better person each day, you will eventually find yourself prepared for the highest version of your vision. It is an amazing journey!

Once you realize your unique vision, it will raise a hunger and passion in you to achieve what God says is possible."
—Bernard Haynes

CHAPTER 4

EXCUSES ARE NOT ACCEPTED. GET THE JOB DONE.

"The sick man answered Him, "Sir, I have no man to put me into the pool when the water is stirred up, but while I am coming, another steps down before me."
— John 5:7

The man at the pool of Bethesda had waited at the pool for thirty-eight long years to receive his healing. Every time he would go to the pool for healing after the angel stirred the water, someone would beat him to the punch. His situation looked impossible.

Making excuses infected this man's life so greatly he could not see his healer standing in front of him. When Jesus asked him if he wanted to be made whole, the first words that came out of his mouth were excuses as to why he could not get to the water to receive his healing.

He told Jesus, "Sir, I have no man to put me into the pool when the water is stirred up, but while I am coming, another steps down before me." (John 5:7). Jesus did not ask him what or who was keeping him from entering the pool. He wanted to know if the man desired to be made whole. The man's excuses could have cost him his healing.

What excuses have kept you from living your vision? Have you told yourself that you are not smart enough to get the promotion, you do not deserve to live a better life, you are not articulate enough to teach, or you will never make enough money to live debt free? Have you convinced yourself with your excuses that living your vision is out of reach?

"Excuses are not accepted. Get the job done." This is one of my favorite quotes of all time. I don't know who gets credit for saying it, but I first heard this quote my senior year playing high school basketball. Our coach gave these inspiring quotes for us to learn and repeat during and after practice for motivation. This quote became our motivating battle cry because of the trials we experienced that year.

We played all of our games on the road because the administration decided to remodel the gym right before the beginning of basketball season. To this day, I still do not understand why. They gave us no respect.

We endured a tough regular season because of the distractions of not having a home gym. We had to practice and play all of our games on the road. I remember carrying two uniforms to some games because we did not know if we were the home or visiting team.

During the regular season, we played hard through all the distractions, but we still ended the season with a losing record. After the regular season, our next game was the sub-regional tournament. We were ranked last in our sub-region. People were expecting us to play one game and lose.

I remember something powerful happening in practice the week before the tournament that changed the remainder of our season. We decided to take our quote seriously, make no excuses and get the job done. We refused to allow our losing record, our last place ranking or our lack of a home gym to keep us from making a real effort to win the tournament.

We turned a potential list of excuses as to why it was okay to lose into motivation to win the tournament. During practice that week, we decided to play like the neutral site was our home gym. We made up our mind that no team that week could beat us. We turned a potential negative situation into positive winning energy.

The first night of the tournament, we played the third-ranked team and won. The next night, we played the second-ranked team and won. In the championship game, we played the number one team and won. We did what others thought was impossible: winning the sub-regional championship.

Our next challenge was the regional playoffs. We knew if we won one game, we would go to the state playoffs. Our intentions were not to just win one game, but to win the regional tournament.

We again set our minds to the thought that this neutral site was our home gym and no team could beat us. We played the first game and won. We knew after that win we were in the state playoffs, but we wanted that regional championship. We accomplished what seemed impossible because we did not allow excuses to cloud our minds on what is possible.

The rest of the story is we lost the regional championship in a very close game. Even though we lost the game, we still went to the state playoffs. In the state playoffs, we lost in the last few seconds of a thrilling first-round game.

It was a very disappointing loss. We had our opportunities to win, but we let them slip through our hands. We gained valuable life lessons that season because we saw what was possible when you work hard and do not allow excuses to control you.

I share this story to challenge you to let go of hindering excuses and go after what you know is possible for your life and family. You do not know what you can accomplish until you do it.

- I do not care if no one has done it before; do it anyway.

- I do not care if no one will go with you; go alone.

- I do not care if you do not get encouragement from your family or friends; encourage yourself.

If God asks you the question, "Do you want to be made whole?" jump up, and tell Him yes, and then do exactly what He tells you to do without any excuses.

"The person who really wants to do something finds a way; the other person finds an excuse."

CHAPTER 5

VISION CHALLENGED

"For forty days the Philistine came forward every morning and
evening and took his stand."
— I Samuel 17:26

Have you ever been challenged by a situation that made you want to quit? Have you ever faced a challenge that made you feel incapable and insufficient?

Israel faced Goliath, an impressive and seemingly unconquerable 10-foot giant (I Samuel 17:8-9). He spent forty days calling out King Saul and the Army of Israel, telling them they did not stand a chance against him. He overwhelmed them with constant fear so that, whenever he came out to challenge them, they would run and hide.

Goliath's intense challenge even had King Saul, the one person who was able to stand against him, hiding in fear. Every morning and every evening for forty days, Goliath presented his challenge to the Army of Israel. For forty days, they lived in fear, intimidated by the giant. For forty days, Goliath flaunted his size and strength, daring Saul to send someone to fight him.

This is how the giants in your life will challenge your vision. Your giants will come at you morning, noon and evening, day after day, relentlessly trying to derail you from living your vision. Their intentions are to steal, kill and literally destroy the vision that lives within you. They will say,

- You can run from your responsibilities.
- You are not worthy to live a blessed life.
- You cannot achieve great things.
- You are condemned because of your past.

Goliath wants you to doubt God's Word for your life. He wants you to give up on your future because of what happened in your life yesterday. He wants to persuade you to trust your flesh instead of trusting the leading of God's vision. He wants you to believe God has forgotten you in the midst of your troubles.

You may be on the verge of quitting. You may be thinking this vision thing is not worth the fight. You may be thinking about walking away from everything, your family, friends, job, church, life and God. I want to admonish you through all the challenges that you must keep moving forward. I truly believe it is not over in your life until God says it is over. If God allows you to see another day, if He permits you to breathe again, then you are responsible for staying in the fight.

Have you ever encountered such extreme pressure that it seemed impossible to endure? Have you ever been in too deep, so that you thought you would never get out? These intense times will either draw you closer to God or draw you farther away. In your times of pressure, always remember, "Greater is He who is in you than he who is in the world." (I John 4:4).

God desires to use your pressure situations to shape you like a priceless diamond. Just as diamonds can only be formed when sufficient pressure and temperatures exist below the ground, you cannot become all God destined you to be without intense pressure in your life.

He allows pressure situations in your life so that you can see His strength and your weakness; His wisdom and your foolishness; His ability and your inability; and His infinite qualities and your finite qualities.

Do not run from your challenges. God knows what you are dealing with. He knows your marriage is struggling; your finances are no longer funny. He knows your health is not good, your children are out of control and your job is downsizing. He knows all of your situations. Can I tell you what else He knows? He knows who He created you to become.

God created you to become a person of purpose, to live a life of victory and to fulfill your vision. You may say, "But you don't understand what I am going through and how long I have dealt with it. I am frustrated and exhausted. I don't believe I will ever attain victory in this situation."

I want you to know that the enemy is a liar; you are victorious because of what I Corinthians 15:57 says: "But thanks be to God which gives us the victory through our Lord Jesus Christ."

Please take notice: the Word of God says victory is through your relationship with Jesus.

- Not your relationship with your family and friends.
- Not the strength of your bank account and retirement portfolio.
- Not the power and prestige of the positions you hold.
- Not in the amount of degrees and work experience you have accumulated.

You gain your ultimate victory to living your vision when you overcome your challenges in His strength.

"The hero is the man who lets no obstacle prevent him from pursuing the values he has chosen."
— Andrew Bernstein

CHAPTER 6

MAKE YOUR VISION A REALITY

"For the dream comes through much effort and the voice of a fool through many words."
— Ecclesiastes 5:3

What dreams have you spent years talking about, but never accomplished? You told yourself and those around you what you were going to do one day. You were excited to tell your dreams to anyone who would listen.

You may have wasted valuable time saying, "One day I am going to start my own business." Or "Next month, I will start a savings plan." Or "Next year, I am going back to school." Seven years, ten jobs and a pile of bills later, you are still saying the same thing. Life is moving, and you are still stuck singing the same old song.

I know this story all too well because it is my story. I realized a few years ago if I am going to live my vision, I must get busy. The one thing you and I can never get back is missed time. Today is the perfect day to stop talking about what you desire to do and start doing it.

You must overcome the fear of failure, rejection, excuses, others' opinions, and procrastination. You must make up your mind to pursue your vision even if you have to do it afraid. If you make the effort to move your vision forward, God will send the necessary resources and people you need to make things happen.

The time is now to make your vision a reality. You will encounter struggle, resistance and opposition, but you can do it. Not everyone who is close to you will understand why you are doing what you are doing, but do it anyway. Sometimes it will take great effort to motivate yourself to move forward, but let faith lead you.

On your journey to making your vision a reality, here are nine motivators to help you succeed.

1. **Evaluate where you are**. Take a close look at how your life is lining up in these seven areas of life (spiritual, relational, physical, mental, financial, social and professional). Knowing where you currently are positions you to see where you need go. If you need to make changes for improvement, do it now and do not wait for tomorrow.

2. **Envision where you desire to be.** See yourself where you have never been, doing what you have never done before and walking in it even in the face of fear. Make sure what you are envisioning aligns with what you are purposed to do and not what someone else envisions for your life.

3. **Establish a clear plan**. Create a clear personal vision statement that documents where you want to go. A vision statement should clearly describe what you want most in life, how you expect to get there and a timeline for making your vision a reality.

4. **Eliminate distractions**. Disassociate with anything or anyone that is an obstacle to where you believe God is leading you. You must diffuse the distractions immediately because they can cause you to forfeit your vision with negative and discouraging talk and actions.

5. **Explore all options**. Look at all your options with wide-open lenses. Focus on your specific vision, but keep your peripheral sight open to all the available options. There is usually more than one way to a destination.

6. **Enlist the help of others.** You cannot possibly make your vision a reality on your own. You will need some assistance. Enlist the help of those who are willing to encourage and walk

with you, even when things do not make sense and they cannot see the reality of your vision.

7. **Execute your vision plan.** Once you have a documented plan, it is time to take action. Do not waste a lot of time telling everyone who will listen about it, but start executing your plan. What good is it to possess a great written vision plan and never take action? When you take action, you unlock the secret to achieving your vision.

8. **Examine your process.** As you take action on your vision, you will need to continually monitor your progress to see where you are and if you are on the right path. Examining your vision process regularly lets you know if you need to make any adjustments or changes.

9. **Enjoy the journey**. I do not want you to think that working to make your vision a reality is all work and no fun. You must implement rewards that follow key steps of vision achievement, because if you do not, you will make your vision journey a burdensome task that will leave you frustrated and discouraged. Rewarding accomplishments makes your vision journey enjoyable and provides a greater incentive to get the job done.

I am implementing these nine motivators in my life as I write this message. If you are serious about making your vision a reality, you can start right where you are by implementing these nine motivators. Then watch what happens.

"With vision, there is no room to be frightened.
No reason for intimidation. It's time to march forward!
Let's be confident and positive!"
— Charles Swindoll

CHAPTER 7

VISION IS THE MISSING INGREDIENT TO ABUNDANT LIVING

"And the Lord answered me, and said write the vision..."
— Habakkuk 2:2

Habakkuk 2:2 is an often-quoted scripture for ministries and churches that desire to move forward with a corporate vision. Yearlong vision campaigns are developed and implemented in conjunction with this verse. Conferences and seminars are created with this verse as the main theme.

I have seen people get excited when they hear this verse proclaimed by a pastor or teacher. They will shout, high-five their neighbors and dance around the sanctuary with great enthusiasm upon the declaration of this word. There have been songs and books written about Habakkuk 2:2. Needless to say, this is a very popular verse when it comes to talking about writing a vision.

It is sad to report that, after hearing this powerful verse proclaimed, many people still have not made the effort or taken the time to write a personal and/or family vision.

It sounds inspiring and motivating to hear a teacher or preacher proclaiming, "Write the vision and make it plain." I have discovered, however, that it takes more than an inspirational message or weekend seminar about vision to make things happen. It takes a concentrated effort to write your vision and an unwavering commitment to implement it.

A few years ago, I came to a point in my life where I desired something different. I had some perplexing questions I wanted to ask God, but felt afraid and intimidated, until I read Habakkuk's story.

Habakkuk was perplexed about the situations happening around him. God's actions confused him. His confusion led him to ask God two key questions: "How long O Lord will I call for help and you will not hear?" and "How can you use the Babylonians who are more sinful than we are to punish us?" Habakkuk needed some real answers to his questions, and only God could provide the answers he needed. (Read Habakkuk 1)

It may come as a shock to you (as it did to me at first) that Habakkuk would boldly ask the God of the universe these questions. You may say, "How could Habakkuk offend God with these questions?" I do not believe God was offended by his inquiry. I believe God would have been offended if he went to others looking for the answer to his questions.

I know this is hard to reconcile for some people, because they were taught not to question God. God wants you to bring your questions and concerns to Him. He wants you to come to Him seeking His face in a humble, honest and sincere manner (not arrogant or prideful.) The sad thing is we often come to Him after exhausting all of our resources and then we want Him to turn our situations around immediately.

One evening, after my family had gone to bed, I went to my room in the basement to ask God some serious questions about my life's direction. As I asked Him the most pressing questions on my heart, He led me to read the book of Habakkuk. After reading the three chapters in Habakkuk several times, it hit me like a ton of bricks: I needed to realize, write and implement God's vision for my life, marriage and family.

That night, I made a commitment to write a vision for every area of my life. Over the next couple of weeks, I sought God's face and He revealed His vision for my life. I wrote my vision in explicit details and immediately started implementing it.

If I can be honest, I have detoured and even failed at times because;

- I allowed fear to dictate my walk.
- I allowed current situations to discourage my progress.
- I missed opportunities because I listened to the creation instead of the creator.

Now is the time to unlock the power of your vision. After spending quality time studying and meditating on Habakkuk 2:1-4, I extrapolated seven keys to unlocking the power of your vision. If you implement these seven keys, your vision will have a powerful impact on your family, friends, community, city, country and the world.

1. Vision is revealed to the person in position to listen.
2. Vision must be written down.
3. Vision must be made plain.
4. Vision must be posted.
5. Vision overcomes obstacles.
6. Vision will manifest itself in God's time.
7. Vision must be lived by faith.

In the next four messages, we will take a detailed look at each of the seven keys. Get ready to unlock your vision and live your life with impact.

"Hold fast to dreams for if dreams die, life is a broken winged bird that cannot fly."
— Langston Hughes

CHAPTER 8

UNLOCKING THE POWER OF YOUR VISION
KEY 1 AND 2

*"I will stand upon my watch, and set me upon the tower and will
watch to see what he will say unto me and what I shall answer when
I am reproved. Then the Lord answered me and said,
record the vision…"*
— Habakkuk 2:1-2

Key #1 –Vision is revealed when you are in position to listen.

For you to unlock the power of your vision from God, you must
first reside in your personal watchtower to listen for His directions.
In ancient times, watchtowers were built on city walls so watchmen
could see their enemies or messengers approaching their city from a
distance.

From the watchtower, they could see the enemy approaching and alert
the people in enough time to prepare for battle. The prophets used the
picture of the watchman and watchtower to emphasize an attitude of
expectation. Habakkuk went to his personal watchtower expecting to
hear from God. He knew this was the place and time to listen to how
God would answer his perplexing questions.

Do you have a personal watchtower where you can hear from God?
Wherever your watchtower may be, (a room in the basement, the
living room after everyone is asleep, an early morning walk or a quiet
place in the park) you must get alone with God. You need to make
sure your time alone with Him is uninterrupted. When you go to your
watchtower, you need to put away your mobile devices, turn off the

television, close your Facebook page and tell your family and friends not to disturb you unless it is a serious emergency.

Your daily time in your personal watchtower is your time to meet with God and hear His directions. You will need to take with you some tools: a Bible to read and study what He says (I recommend the New King James Version or the New American Standard Bible.); a pen and paper (Take a journal or our Vision Impact Workbook to record what He speaks into your life.); and an open and receptive ear to listen to His guidance.

You do not have to come with any games or gimmicks. You do not have to worry about the right words to say or a special prayer formula. You do not have to line up all your ducks in a row or possess all the correct answers. You can come to Him in an honest, humble and specific way to let Him know what is on your heart and mind. When you share your heart's deepest desires, the God of the universe will respond with His directions for your life and/or family.

Key #2 – Vision must be written down.

You need a clear vision that belongs to you and directs your life. You cannot be valuable to God's ultimate plan if you do not know and understand your personal vision. Whether you are young, old, married, single, middle-aged, black or white, if you do not have a clearly written vision, the circumstances of life will easily distract, discourage and disappoint you.

You learned from the first key th atyou have to get alone with God in your personal watchtower to hear from Him. Habakkuk received a vision of what would eventually happen to the Babylonians while he was in his watchtower. God did not instruct Habakkuk to think, pray and talk about the vision, but He specifically told him to write the vision He would reveal. God knew a written vision would solidify it in the heart and mind of the people.

God's vision is not based upon what you have or do not have. It does not matter what others say or do not say. It does not matter how much money you have or do not have. It does not matter if you are the CEO or the janitor.

You may not totally understand everything God is revealing to you; it may not make much sense, but write it down anyway. What you write down may not match your current situation. What you write down may seem unachievable. What you write down may look crazy to others and even you. You may even second-guess your abilities and talents.

You must believe that if God said it you can take it to the bank and cash it. He may give you a plan to pay off your debt even though you are broke. He may give you a plan for a business even though you do not have the necessary experience. He may give you a plan for a successful marriage while you are still single. Whatever He reveals to you, write it down and start moving toward it.

Today is the right day to begin writing your personal and/or family vision statement. Your vision statement is what God reveals to you and not what you receive from someone's insight, book or seminar. I encourage you to write your vision in explicit details.

Do not leave anything out because you feel inadequate or incapable because of the enormity of the vision. Please know God's vision will be bigger than what you can do or handle in your own strength. His vision can intimidate you. It can make you feel inept and look foolish. Your abilities and skills can look insufficient. But, when He reveals your vision to you it is your responsibility to put it into action.

"Most of the successful people I've known are the ones who do more listening than talking."
— Bernard M. Baruch

CHAPTER 9

UNLOCKING THE POWER OF YOUR VISION
KEYS 3 AND 4

"... and make it plain upon tables that he may run that reads it..." —
Habakkuk 2:2

Key #3 – Vision must be plain.

After spending the necessary time writing your vision, you need to make sure it is written in plain, simple to understand language. You want your vision so plain a fifth grader can understand it. I have read complex and convoluted vision statements that left people confused and discouraged because they lacked focus and clear direction.

They were well-written statements with impressive and inspirational words and phrases, but they lacked real direction to motivate people to move. The vision statements were so complicated that the individual with the vision could not really explain it in a way others could grasp it and run with it.

If you have a vision that is not easily grasped by the people connected to it, they will not follow it and will end up creating an alternate vision to follow.

When Habakkuk received his vision from God, he wrote it in plain and understandable terms for all the Israelites and future generations to see. The vision is recorded in scripture to provide a roadmap for how to write a vision statement.

An effective vision statement that is plain and understandable will equip and empower your future generation with the tools it needs to excel. When your great-great-great grandchildren read your vision, they will plainly understand its directions and continue to run with it.

We can sometimes over-complicate things because we either think we are smarter than we actually are, or we are trying to impress others. A vision statement that is written in plain, understandable language will energize and inspire everyone connected to it so that they will run with eager anticipation.

Key #4 – Vision must be posted.

If you walk into the entrance of some companies and ministries, you will see a posted vision statement. This posted vision statement gives the direction for the organization. Everyone who enters the company or ministry knows that there is a clear and definite direction. Most of all, the posted vision statement gives direction and unifies everyone connected to it. This is very important because it puts everyone on the same page. No one is left in the dark about the direction of the organization.

Just as a business or ministry posts its vision statement, you need to visibly post your vision statement to keep you and everyone connected to it progressing in the same direction. When everyone is on the same page, it brings a greater level of clarity, responsibility and accountability.

After you have written your vision statement in plain, understandable terminology, it is now time to post it. I suggest typing it on a one-page summary sheet that you can frame. Once you frame your vision statement, place it in an ideal location, so that it is visible every day. Or, if it is a family vision, place it in a prominent place where your entire family can see and read it.

Use it as a screen saver on your computer or mobile device. Write your vision on an index card, laminate it and carry it in your wallet or purse. Post it on your refrigerator so that every time you or someone opens it, they will see the vision.

Wherever you need to, post your vision. Your posted vision statement is your constant reminder of what is possible in your life and/or family if you follow God's directions. It becomes your encourager and motivator to move forward whenever you are discouraged, distracted or disappointed by life.

"One of the marks of successful people is that they are action-oriented. One of the marks of average people is that they are talk-oriented."
— Brian Tracy

CHAPTER 10

UNLOCKING THE POWER OF YOUR VISION KEYS 5 AND 6

"For the vision is yet for the appointed time. It hastens toward the goal and it will not fail. Though it tarries, wait for it. For it will certainly come, it will not delay."
— Habakkuk 2:3

Key #5 – Vision overcomes obstacles.

Do not think because God gives you a clear vision your life is going to be smooth sailing. You will encounter some overwhelming obstacles. You will experience some unforeseeable turbulence. You will have days you want to throw in the towel and walk away from everything.

The enemy will use every tactic in his arsenal to detour your destiny. He will use your friends, family, coworkers and even yourself against you. His ultimate job is to steal, kill and destroy your vision (John 10:10).

He will speak discouraging commentary into your ear like, "Don't you know where you come from? No one is going to listen to you. Why try and do this because you failed the last time?" The enemy wants you to walk away from your commitments. He wants you to live inconsistently to your purpose. He knows if he can keep you distracted from living your vision's full potential then you will not impact your family, community and city the way God designed for you.

Not only will the enemy present obstacles to your vision, but others will try to dissuade you from advancing forward. They will say things like, "How are you going to accomplish that with your education or skill set? That has never been done before in your family. You know you are too old or young to make that happen?" Do not let what others say determine your destiny. Do not let them talk you out of God's promises for your life. Turn a deaf ear to their negative words and focus on your vision.

A major obstacle to living your vision you will have to overcome is yourself. You and I will talk ourselves out of our vision. We will say what we cannot do instead of saying, "I can do everything God designed me to do". We will say we cannot accomplish something because of our background or lack of experience. Instead, we need to say, "I am going to learn and do what I need to and God will take care of the rest".

When fear and worry attempts to dissuade you, you need to say, "God did not give me the spirit of fear, but of power, love and a sound mind." (II Timothy 1:7) When you turn your attention in the direction of your vision instead of your problems, you can walk in the assurance that victory is possible.

God designed your life to be motivated and fueled by His vision. You do not have to run and hide from life's challenges. You do not have to live a mediocre existence. You do not have to down play who you are. You can pursue your vision with an aggressive, offensive attack that will equip and empower you to overcome any obstacles that stand in your way.

Key #6 – Vision manifests itself in God's time.

Habakkuk waited patiently for his vision. God revealed to him, He would use the wicked Babylonians to punish Judah. He would allow the Babylonians to rule for a season, but in due time they would be punished for their wickedness. Habakkuk teaches us the all-important virtue of waiting.

God desires for us to know through Habakkuk's vision we are to cherish our waiting period. Though it may take a while before your vision unfolds, you are to use your waiting period as a time to grow in knowledge and walk in wisdom. Your waiting period is your proving ground to make the necessary preparations you need because when your vision begins to manifest itself, you want to be ready to operate in it.

Please do not rush your vision. Be patient. When you make your own plans to execute, you force those plans into your own timetable and can possibly delay your destiny. Vision manifests when God determines the time. When the time is right, God will unveil your vision progressively. I know from experience waiting takes patience. The difficulty of patience surfaces when you see the possibilities, but it seems things are moving in molasses.

You may have written your vision in explicit details. You may have followed it to the letter, but it seems nothing is working out. It seems the more you work towards your vision, the more difficult it gets. The more attacks you encounter, the more aggravated and frustrated you become. You may get to the point that you just want to bail out. You want to tell God, He can have this vision because it isn't worth the time and energy.

Whether it is going back to school, exercising more days a week, turning off the television and reading or learning a new area at work, you must make the necessary adjustments to bring your vision forth. You are going to have to work on your vision when others are playing, sleeping and having a good time.

You are going to have to make some sacrifices that will cost you something in the short term. Hang in there because your release is coming soon. You cannot quit when your vision journey becomes a little uncomfortable. You cannot walk away when the road gets bumpy just know the finish line is in front of you.

Your revealed vision will inspire you to look beyond your waiting process and see your future promise. Now, when I talk about waiting, I am not talking about waiting like at a bus stop. At a bus stop, you just stand waiting on the next bus to arrive. When I talk about waiting, I am talking about waiting like a server at a restaurant.

A good server is constantly moving, serving the customers he is responsible for taking care of. If he wants a good tip, he makes sure his customers are properly served. He does not stop making sure their drinks are filled and their food is properly prepared. He continues to provide excellent service until the customers leave.

The server anticipates at the end of the meal, if he provided superb service, he knows he stands a great chance of getting an excellent tip. Even if he does not get the tip he thinks he deserves, when the next customer comes he gives the same excellent service anticipating a good tip. Just as a server is anticipating a good tip from the excellent service he gives, it is crucial we serve in excellence anticipating receiving the rewards of our vision in this present life and the life to come.

"You are not here merely to make a living. You are here to enable the world to live more amply, with greater vision, and with finer spirit of hope and achievement. You are here to enrich the world. You impoverish yourself if you forget this errand."
— Woodrow Wilson

CHAPTER 11

UNLOCKING THE POWER OF YOUR VISION
KEY 7

*"Behold, as for the proud one, His soul is not right within him; but
the righteous will live by his faith."*
— Habakkuk 2:4

Key #7 –Vision is lived by faith.

Habakkuk had total faith in the vision God revealed to him. He
declared to the people that the God of the universe would spare them
from the ruthless reign of the Babylonians. God assured him that
the wicked Babylonians, who trusted in their abilities and strengths,
would eventually fall (Habakkuk 2:5-20). Habakkuk's job was to keep
encouraging the people to live by faith while they waited patiently for
the vision to come to pass.

If you operate your vision by sight, you will always see the potential
problems and pain that may surface. Seeing your problems and pain
from a physical viewpoint may cause you to deviate from pursuing
your vision. You may see you have more month than money. You may
see friends who said they had your back bail on you. You may witness
the economy and job market improving for others, but not for you.

Life is full of potential discouraging and depressing circumstances
that can keep you living life on the sidelines. However, when you
decide to live your vision by faith, you can move from the sidelines to
playing in the game.

One definition of vision is seeing farther than your physical eyes can
see. It was hard for the people of Judah to see their deliverance when

the Babylonians ruthlessly reigned and ruled over them. How could they see a vision of victory while they were encountering tremendous defeat from their enemy? The only way they could possibly see a vision for victory was through the eyes of faith.

If you are enduring difficult times and are discouraged, if you have lost the desire for your vision due to constant struggles or if you have allowed your circumstances to derail you, you must take an active role in regaining your faith for your vision. God gave you a vision so you would trust Him and not just trust what you see. When you begin to see your vision with the eyes of faith, you understand the obstacles you see are only temporary.

Habakkuk realized through the eyes of God's vision that the Babylonians reign was temporary. Though it was going to be a difficult time for the Israelites under the harsh leadership of the Babylonians, they could live through it by faith in God's vision.

Habakkuk was so in tuned with his faith in the vision that in Habakkuk 3; he praised God for the victory they would eventually experience over the Babylonians. Faith in your vision is paramount because the way you see your vision determines how you think, what you say and when you act.

The more you focus your attention on your vision the more your faith grows. Taking slow and steady faith steps on your vision journey opens the door for more opportunities for success to come your way.

If you choose instead to walk by fear, you will waste time and energy on activities that takes you away from your unique vision course. If you choose to activate your faith, you will courageously move forward in following your promised path to sure vision success.

"You can't change the past, but you can ruin the present by worrying about the future."
— Unknown

CHAPTER 12

DO YOU HAVE SIGHT OR VISION?

"Commit your way to the LORD; trust also in Him;
and He will do it."
— Psalm 37:5

I have opened several seminars and workshops by holding a pinecone in my hand and asking the participants, "What do you see?" Without fail, people shout, "A pinecone." I ask them the same question again. They look at me with bewilderment in their eyes and say, with reservation, "A pinecone." I ask them the same question a third time. When I ask the third time, I get confused looks and usually no responses.

Before I give them the answer, I share with them my pinecone experience. I share the story of the day I was cutting grass and complaining to God about why I was struggling in several areas of my life. I had stopped cutting grass to move some pinecones out of the way. As I picked up the cones, it was as if I heard the voice of God say, "What are you holding?" Of course I said, "A pinecone."

I heard the same question again and I gave the same exact answer, "A pinecone." I heard the same question a third time and I was confused as to what the correct answer should be. Honestly, I became angry, because it was hot, I was tired and I felt God was playing with me. I guess this is the way the participants in my seminars feel when I ask them a seemingly easy question three times.

I looked at the pinecone again and I was about to throw it in the woods when I noticed something. I saw several pine trees in my backyard. I looked at the pinecone again and a light bulb went off. This one pinecone had the potential to produce all of the pine trees that were in my backyard. Not only did this one pinecone have the potential to produce all the pine trees, but also everything in the woods could be directly or indirectly connected to a single pinecone.

I expanded my thinking, beyond the pinecone, to the woods in my back yard. I saw, contained within one pinecone, the potential for an entire forest. If you think about it, the pinecone is a seed that contains a potential tree and that tree contains more pinecones, which produces more trees. Those trees produce more seeds, and the process continues as long as there are seeds being produced, until you have a forest.

I was totally blown away by my discovery. I realized that day that I had been living by sight instead of vision. I had great sight for things I could see and put my hands on, but I could see no farther. My vision was obstructed because I could not see beyond my current situation. I was looking at my situations through the eyes of my finite sight, instead of the eyes of God's vision.

When I finish sharing my experience about the pinecone with the seminar participants, nearly everyone's eyes are wide open, because they see the picture. They see that the vision of the pinecone is much bigger than what it appears to be through the physical eyes. They realize the only way you can see a forest from a pinecone is through the eyes of vision.

Have you been operating your life by sight or vision? Vision is the source and hope of life. One of the greatest gifts God gave to mankind is the gift of vision. What could possibly be more satisfying than to know the God of the universe wants you to operate your life by His vision and not by your physical sight? No invention, product, accomplishment, or universe was accomplished without the inspiring power of vision. Vision is the engine that drives progress.

Operating by sight can cause you to see the problems and challenges around you instead of the solutions God equipped and empowered you with. You see the stack of bills, the near negative bank account, the downturn in the economy, struggles at home and the decline in the job market. Sight without vision is dangerous because it can cause you to see no hope for a better future.

Think about the pinecone. There is incredible potential, possibility and power that lives within the pinecone. Can I let you in on a secret? The same thing is true of you. God has placed within you the potential of turning your seed (purpose) into a thriving, powerful and productive vision that will change your life and positively affect the lives of everyone connected to you.

My experience with the pinecone that day opened me to five truths that will help you move from sight to vision.

1. Sight is a function of the eyes, while vision is a function of faith.

2. Sight is the ability to see things as they are, while vision is the ability to see things as they could or should be.

3. Sight is confined to your current environment, while vision sees beyond your now to your future possibilities.

4. Sight is based upon what your eyes determine to be true; while vision focuses on what God's Word says is true.

5. Sight is fueled by an idea that will bring temporary satisfaction, while vision is fueled by an idea so powerful that it can live beyond the grave.

"Relying on what you see with your physical eyes can blind you from seeing your future possibilities."
— Bernard Haynes

CHAPTER 13

WRITE YOUR VISION

"Without a written vision and a plan to achieve it, you will never live to your full potential."
— Bernard Haynes

We can spend more time planning a one-week vacation or what we are going to wear for a night on the town than identifying what outcomes we want to see in the major areas of our lives. This kind of mindset can lead a person to wander aimlessly from day to day, week to week and year to year with no clear direction in mind. For this reason, it is necessary that everyone should take the time to create a written vision plan to give his life direction.

A personal vision statement is your GPS that guides you to the destination that God designed for your life. It ensures that you stay focused on your plan and do not get involved with anything or anyone that will sidetrack you from your vision course. It is your guiding light to lead you through the storms and obstacles that will challenge your direction.

Don't let the enormity of a vision dissuade you from writing it down and taking action. I encourage you to write your vision statement in explicit details. Don't leave anything out. Don't let others discourage you. Don't let your present situation detour you.

Please know that God's vision for your life is not based upon:

- What you have or do not have.
- What others say or do not say.

- How much money you have or do not have.
- Whether you are the CEO or the janitor.
- Whether you completely understand it or not.

It is based upon who God determined you to be and what He assigned you to do in this present time.

Here are seven reasons why you need a written vision plan:

1. **It empowers you to clarify your life's direction.** The CEO has a business plan to guide the company. A football coach has a game plan to lead his team. A builder uses a blueprint to construct a house.

   A written vision plan empowers you to construct and clarify your life. It gives you the correct directions and coordinates to follow. It gives you the inspiration and motivation you need to move forward, even in the face of fear. If you don't have a written vision, it is time to sit down and start developing one.

2. **It allows you to guard your life against imbalances.** A written vision plan helps you focus on the things essential to living your destiny. It helps you maintain a healthy balance between where you are and where you desire to go.

   Some people sacrifice their family for a career. Others sacrifice their health for temporary pleasure or a nurturing relationship with their children for worldly success. If you want a healthy marriage, a successful career, productive children, stable finances or good health, it is possible, if you have a clearly written vision plan that maintains a cohesive balance with all the areas of your life.

3. **It helps you filter the distractions.** A filter is a device used to extract impurities from air or water. A written vision plan can be described as a filter that extracts the distractions and discouragements that interfere with your life's direction.

A written vision plan allows you to say "yes" to what matters most and "no" to those activities detrimental to your vision. It will give you the clarity and confidence you need to make the most of your potential opportunities. What distractions to living your vision do you need to filter?

4. **It aids you in identifying where you are.** A written vision not only points you to the future, but it helps you identify where you are so you can get to where you desire to be.

   You may have to acknowledge that you need to make external and internal life changes. You may realize that you must make immediate changes to your present position to open opportunities for a better future.

5. **Identifying where you are helps you evaluate** the direction of your vision against the backdrop of your current realities. When you are honest about your current realities, your written vision will empower you with the right instructions and inspiration you need to make right decisions.

6. **It equips you to move toward a better future.** A ship that sets sail for an island destination is equipped with a compass that navigates its direction, a rudder to help the pilot steer the ship and a plan to set course to its destination. In the same way, a written vision becomes your compass, rudder and plan to direct your steps toward a better future.

   When you are equipped to move toward your destined future, your focus will shift from yesterday's problems to today's possibilities for tomorrow's promises. What do you desire for your future (spiritually, relationally, physically, socially, mentally, financially and professionally)?

   It serves as your road map. Back in the day, we used road maps to get us to our destinations. With today's technological advances the road map changed from a printed map to a GPS.

A GPS gives you the directions you need in seconds. If the directions change, it recalibrates within a few seconds to give an alternate route.

7. **Your vision plan acts as a GPS for your life.** Please know that you will hit some potholes and encounter roadblocks. But your vision gives you the turns and alternate routes you need to take to get you to your ultimate destination. Being clear on where you want to be is deeply important, and pursuing it passionately helps you grow and develop into the person God designed you to be.

It inspires you to focus forward without holding on to past regrets. The World is waiting for you to make an impact with your vision. Many people live with debilitating regrets because life is not turning out the way they anticipated. They live daily with disappointment, discontentment and discouragement, but it doesn't have to be this way. You do not have to let past regrets hold you hostage from living a better life.

We have all experienced something from our past that, if we had the opportunity for a redo, we would do differently. The reality is you do not get an opportunity for a redo. You can strive not to repeat the sins and mistakes from your past. If you start focusing on your present life for a better future, you won't waste time holding on to past regrets.

While you cannot control everything that happens in your life, you can take the time to write and implement a vision plan. A written and implemented vision plan will dramatically improve your chances of ending up at the destination God designed for you.

"Never interrupt someone doing what you said couldn't be done."
— Amelia Earhart

CHAPTER 14

IN PURSUIT OF PURPOSE

*"The purposes of a man's heart are deep waters, but a man of
understanding draws them out."*
— *Proverbs 20:5*

Are you clear about your life's purpose? God did not meticulously design you to live a haphazard life full of frustration and confusion. He created you with a unique purpose to pursue. Without purpose, you will never experience the level of fulfillment that is possible for your life.

Purpose is your unique life assignment designed by God. It provides the direction for your daily living and the foundation for your values, vision and goals. It gives meaning to everything you do in your personal, family, social, financial and professional life.

Purpose is bigger than your job, career or what you do. It is a calling. It is a mission. It is an overall theme for your life that transcends your daily activities.

Your life purpose is unique to you. No one else in the world can fulfill your purpose but you. Whether it concerns an area explored by many or by only a few, what matters is that no one can approach it the way you can.

If you have not experienced the level of success you know you are capable of or if you have felt as if something is missing from your life, take note of this very important principle. You will only experience true success in your life to the extent you are clear about your life's purpose.

God created you with the desire to pursue your purpose. Without it, you are paralyzed by stagnation, crippled by fear, bored by the daily routine or frustrated by failure. Our inherent need for purpose gives rise to questions such as, "Who am I?" "Why am I here?" or "What is the point to life?"

As God begins to reveal the answers to these questions, you will learn that your purpose will not just magically happen. It will not progress forward without your full participation. You must pursue it with a tireless, dedicated work ethic. You are responsible for the intentional fulfillment of your purpose so the world may benefit from your contributions.

When you realize your life's purpose, everything changes. Your desires, the way you approach life, the people you associate with, the material you read and the things you listen to will change to help bring your purpose into proper focus.

When your deepest needs are met, you feel encouraged, empowered and energized. This focus gives rise to greater clarity about who you are, what you stand for and where you are going. A sense of inspired action will naturally rise up inside of you when you are living passionately with clear direction and purpose.

You may ask, "How do I discover my life's purpose?

1. Seek the Creator
First, you have to connect with the creator of the universe. You may have to slow down, change direction and seek after Him. He promises to come to those who search for Him with all their hearts.

> *"You will seek Me and find Me when you search for*
> *Me with all your heart."*
> *— Jeremiah 29:13*

2. Learn about Him

Second, you need to learn about Him. You must gain an understanding of how He thinks. God has a much higher way of thinking than you and I. He desires to teach you to think the way He thinks. He wants you to learn to live your purpose with power.

Failure, lack, worry, fear and defeat are not part of His vocabulary and He does not want them to be a part of yours! The best way to renew your mind to His way of thinking is to read and meditate on His Word, pray daily and listen to empowering messages about Him!

"And do not be conformed to this world, but be transformed by the renewing of your mind..."
— Romans 12:1

3. Spend quality time with the Master

The third step is to spend quality time with the Master daily. Just like in any relationship, you have to invest time and effort to get to know God intimately to hear and know His directions. It is only then that God will reveal His plans to you.

"Commit to the LORD whatever you do, and he will establish your plans."
— Proverbs 16:3

4. Obey His directions

The fourth step is to follow what He reveals to you. You can gain all the knowledge in the world about your purpose, but it will never have the impact God designed it to have until you activate it. Don't sit on your purpose waiting for God to move, He has done all He is going to do.

It is up to you to listen to Him, believe His word and obey His directions. What He says may go against your conventional thinking, your current situation or what others think, but please know obeying

His directions will ultimately lead you on the right path to living out your purpose.

> *"But prove yourselves doers of the word, and not merely hearers who delude themselves."*
> *— James 1:22*

Listen carefully! Your response to God's purpose is the single most transforming event in your life and all else flows from it. This will be the most important exploration you will ever make and the rewards are great: more joy, fulfillment, success and meaning in your life.

> **"What lies behind us and what lies before us are tiny matters compared to what lies within us."**
> **— Oliver Wendell Holmes**

CHAPTER 15

"WHERE ARE YOU?"

*"Then the Lord God called to the man and said to him,
'Where are you?'"*
— Genesis 3:9

When God asked Adam, "Where are you?" He knew exactly where Adam was. He knew he had deliberately disobeyed His command against eating the forbidden fruit. Adam's guilt and fear caused him to attempt to hide from God. All God wanted him to do was to be upfront and honest with Him and come clean about what he had done.

I believe it would have been a different outcome if Adam had sought God for forgiveness. I believe God would have bestowed His restoring favor on him and Eve. God was waiting for Adam to tell Him where he was and what he had done. This was Adam's opportunity to reflect God's character. Instead, he ran and tried to hide from the all-knowing God.

God gave Adam the ultimate plan for his life. He made for him a lovely place where he could live in true peace and prosperity. He placed him in a remarkable garden full of trees that produced fruit: fruit that was beautiful to see and delicious to eat. Everything that God gave him in this wonderful garden was for his enjoyment.

The most incredible thing that took place in the Garden of Eden was that God himself would come to the garden and have intimate fellowship with the man He meticulously created with his hands and in His image. Adam had the hook-up. However, just as we sometimes do, he made a bad decision that cost him dearly. What bad decisions have you made that cost you?

God placed within every person a purpose to pursue and a vision to fulfill. Often we can make terrible decisions that detour our destiny. One of the realities of disobedience is that it separates us from God and takes us off the path to living our vision.

Instead of going right, we listen to our flesh and go left; or when we should go straight, we listen to others' opinions and go down the wrong path. Instead of obeying what we know is right, we do what brings joy to our flesh. When we make the choice to disobey God's direction and follow our flesh, our vision becomes distorted.

If you are outside of God's plan for your life, stop what you are doing and ask for His forgiveness so He can restore you and guide you back on the right path. Even if you blew it, God can put you back better than you were before. When He puts your life back on track, He begins by giving you a greater sense of purpose. You stop making excuses, blaming others and hiding in fear.

- Your purpose becomes clearer.
- Your life becomes energized.
- Your internal man becomes filled with joy.

When faced with the question, "Where are you?" you can boldly tell God where you are and what you need. You do not have to hide or be afraid because He is there to help you. You no longer have to blame your job, your family, your spouse, the government, society or God. You can accept responsibility and get on track to living the life that you were designed to live.

It is the trick of the enemy to make you think that running from God is the answer. The enemy is out to steal, kill and destroy the destiny God designed for your life. He is after your self-esteem, your identity, your mind, your emotions, your plans, your witness and your productivity. He is after everything you value and hold onto as good.

God desires an intimate relationship and loving fellowship with His creation. Adam and Eve were ashamed and embarrassed to face God, and their guilty conscience influenced them to attempt to hide from an all-knowing God. Because of their blatant disobedience, they were afraid to come to Him for restoration.

Disobedience broke their fellowship and hindered their relationship, just as it does with us. God loved Adam and Eve so much that He restored them. He loves us enough that, through Christ, a way has been made for us to renew and restore our relationship and fellowship with Him.

God is calling, "(**Your name**), where are you?" Stop making excuses. Stop procrastinating. Stop allowing yourself to be intimidated by those who say you cannot make it.

Listen to God! Take heed to His directions! He provides everything you need to execute His plan for your life. He has everything set up for you, but He is waiting on you. He is waiting for you to trust Him. He is waiting for your faith to connect with His purpose. He is waiting for you to tell Him where you are, so He can put you on the right road to your destiny.

"Though no one can go back and make a brand new start, anyone can start from now and make a brand new ending."
— Carl Bard

CHAPTER 16

WHO ARE YOU?

"Before I formed you in the womb I knew you, and before you were born I consecrated you; I have appointed you a prophet to the nations."
— Jeremiah 1:5

You can get into serious trouble if you do not have a clear definition of who you are. In our fast-paced, technologically savvy, consumer-driven, twenty-first century world, we have confused our cultural, social and traditional roles with who we truly are. We allow consumer marketing and branding strategies from corporations across the world to influence decisions about what to spend our money on, where to spend our time and who we should emulate.

You will never be satisfied living a life not designed for you. God created you to be an original piece in His overall vision. You are unique. You are a masterpiece. You were customized with a vision only you can carry out.

There are over seven billion people in the world. Of those more than seven billion people, no one has your fingerprints. No one has the material you were designed with. You are not a carbon copy of anyone. You are an original. When God created you, He destroyed the mold so there would never be another person in the world like you.

You cannot afford to waste valuable time and energy trying to imitate anyone else; God wants you to be you. If you are not you, then who is going to be you? Who is going to make the contributions to the world only you can make? You were designed to live your vision. Not your mama's vision. Not your daddy's vision. Not your friend's vision. Not your pastor's vision. Not the media's or someone else's vision.

God made it clear to Jeremiah that He had a very specific vision for him to fulfill. He was designated a prophet to the nations. God did not appoint him as a shepherd, prince or king. He appointed Jeremiah to carry His word forth unto His people. Even though the people would reject what he had to say, he still had to carry out God's assignment.

Just as God had a specific vision for Jeremiah, He has one for you. His vision is so specific to you that, if anyone else tries to live it, he or she will fail. He customized you with a unique vision that is not like anyone else's; accept it and start living your life with excellence.

If you go to a tailor to get a custom suit designed for you, the tailor will take measurements for your body size and dimension. He takes the necessary time to make sure everything is cut and sewn to your distinct body proportions. If any problems arise, he will call you back to re-measure so that everything is properly sized.

When the suit is finished, you will have a product customized to fit only you. If another person tries to wear your suit, it will not fit him properly because it was designed to fit your body dimensions. It may look from a distance like the suit fits, but upon closer investigation, you will discover it does not fit properly.

The suit was custom made for you, and not bought from a department store rack where there could be six suits of the same style, color and size. You are not from the suit rack of a department store. God tailor-made you to fit your unique vision.

Many people assume that, because life seems to work for a neighbor, friend, co-worker or some self-help guru, then the same steps should automatically work for them. They follow tirelessly expecting similar results. Usually this leads to frustration because the way life works for one person is not necessarily the way it will work for someone else.

I am not saying that you do not listen to other people's perspectives or the life processes they went through. You listen because you can glean wisdom from them on what to do and not to do. I believe life's greatest lesson is to learn from someone else's errors and not make the same mistakes.

What another person went through is unique to him or her. The process he went through to get him to where his is may have caused you to walk away from your promise. He was able to go through his process the way he went through it because he was designed for it.

Please know the process you go through is unique to you. No one can go through it for you. Your momma or daddy can't do it for you. Your wife or husband can't do it for you. Your mentor or coach can't do it for you. Your pastor or teacher can't do it for you. You must go through your process for yourself.

If you are trying to be who God has not called you to be, then you are attempting to do things in your own strength and it will not work. You may get away with it for a while, but in the long term, it only leads to frustration and burn-out.

I personally tried for a couple of years to be a church administrator, but no amount of trying and praying worked. I was tired and frustrated because I was doing something I was not ultimately designed to do. I was trying to please man instead of God. I realized I had to face the fact being a church administrator was not part of His vision for my life. He purposed me to be who I am: an encourager and motivator.

You may have to admit you are not who you are trying to be. You may have to face reality that what you are doing has not worked and will never work. You have to decide enough is enough. You have to become sick and tired of being sick and tired of yourself and where you are.

You must determine in your mind to start living the life God designed for you. You may have to honestly say, "God, I need your help because I do not know who I am or where I am going." When you admit you need help, God begins the process of revealing to you who you truly are.

"To be yourself in a world that is constantly trying to make you something else is the greatest accomplishment."
— Ralph Waldo Emerson

CHAPTER 17

IN POSITION FOR PURPOSE

*"And they took him and threw him into the pit. Now the pit was
empty, without any water in it."*
— Genesis 37:24

A couple of years ago I became curious about what it took for a
professional basketball team to become a repeat champion. I researched
professional basketball champions over the last thirty years to find out
what characteristics make repeat champions.

I discovered from my research teams that won multiple championships
possessed players and coaches who understood their position on the
team. Each player knew what his main responsibility and role was
in making his or her team champions. They made a commitment as
a unified team that everyone would play his position at a high level
every game.

They decided to put the team above the individual. This required
each player to give up his personal success for the team. This kind of
dedication and commitment took a major adjustment in their thinking.
For some players, it took a transformation in how they approached
and played each game. The players from repeat championship teams
understood that when the team wins, everyone wins.

I learned from my study of these multiple championship teams that
there are seven key positions (point guard, shooting guard, power
forward, small forward, center, sixth man and coach) that must be
performed in every game with excellence.

The more I studied these teams, the more I became enamored with their approach to winning. What I loved about these teams is that not one player got outside of his position of purpose. If he did, he was quickly reminded that the ultimate mission was to win a championship. Each player, over time, learned to play within his purpose on the team. In other words, the point guard did not try to play the center's position, nor did the center try to play the point guard's position.

I realized when everyone knows and understands his position and performs it at his best, the team can achieve great results. The results for these basketball teams were championships. They became great teams and great champions.

From studying these repeat champions, I began to see in my life that if I focus on my purpose and live according to the way God designed me, then I can achieve success His way. I understand my purpose is not just for me, but it is for everyone who God connects to me.

Joseph was an excellent example of an individual who understood his purpose, even in the midst of very difficult situations. The dream God gave him (in Genesis 37) of ruling over his brothers and father caused him a great deal of turmoil. The beginning of his turmoil resulted in his brothers throwing him in a pit. But he did not allow any of the turmoil he encountered to dissuade him from living his purpose. When he was thrown into the pit, he kept looking up.

As a slave in Potiphar's house, Joseph's character remained strong, and positioned him for greatness. When Potiphar's wife made repeated sexual advances toward him, he remained committed to his purpose. When he was thrown in prison, he consistently lived his purpose and found favor with the warden, guards and inmates. When the butler forgot him and he remained in prison for two more years, his confidence in his purpose did not fail.

When Joseph stood before Pharaoh to interpret his dream, he stood boldly and communicated the purpose for Pharaoh's dreams. His courage to interpret the king's dream without fear opened the door for his promotion to Prime Minister of Egypt. Throughout Joseph's life, he displayed a concentrated effort that kept him in tune to God's purpose in spite of his current situations.

After studying the key positions on repeat basketball championship teams and the life of Joseph, I realized seven key positions of purpose for life. I matched the seven key positions of a repeat championship basketball team with the seven key positions of purpose for life and here are my results.

1. **Coach** – Communicates the organization's vision to the team. You must effectively communicate your purpose to those connected to you through verbal and nonverbal actions.

2. **Point Guard-** Concentrates on leading the team on the court. You must remain concentrated (focused) so you direct your thoughts, attention and actions toward your desired purpose.

3. **Shooting Guard** – Consistently needs to hit key shots. You must consistently demonstrate a reliable, dependable and coherent approach to daily living that aligns your life with your purpose.

4. **Power Forward** – Courage to be the physical player who gives up his body for the sake of the team. You must exhibit courage to stand when everyone else wants to run and to act when everyone is paralyzed by fear.

5. **Small Forward** – Confidence to guard the opponent's best player. You must present authentic confidence and complete reliance in the abilities and gifts God entrusted you with to accomplish your purpose.

6. **Center** – Character to be the strong force in the middle. Your character is who you are when no one is looking and what you are willing to stand for when everyone is looking.

7. **6th Man** – Commitment to coming off the bench. You must make a commitment with your heart, mind and emotions that moves you on a direct course of action in pursuing your purpose.

I know there are more positions to your purpose, but after intense prayer and study, I believe these seven are vitally important in fulfilling your God-designed purpose. Notice I said God-designed purpose and not man- or self-designed. If you apply these seven positions of purpose in your daily life, then you will see your purpose prosper and your life excel.

"The ultimate measure of a man is not where he stands in moments of comfort and convenience, but where he stands at times of challenge and controversy."
— Dr. Martin Luther King, Jr.

CHAPTER 18

KEEP YOUR EYES ON YOUR PRIZE

"If the Lord delights in us, then he will bring us into this land and give us a land flowing with milk and honey."
— Numbers 14:8

Where are your eyes focused? What obstacles have you allowed to block your view of your prize? It is time to remove the distractions, refocus your eyes and pursue your vision at all costs.

When you pursue God's vision for your life, you must keep your eyes focused on your prize. What is the prize? It is a goal that God places in your heart and mind to accomplish, and you will pursue it despite any obstacles or opposition.

The journey may be difficult and discouraging; do not turn around. People will tell you that it cannot be done; do it any way. Obstacles may block your view of your prize; do not give up. If you have to go by yourself, you can make it. When you determine in your mind to focus on your prize, you position and empower yourself to go after everything God assigned to you.

Caleb and Joshua were the two spies in Numbers 13 who believed they could conquer the giants that inhabited their Promised Land. They understood the significance of keeping their eyes on the prize. They did not care how great or big the giants in the land were; they knew they served a bigger God. They saw the greatness and the prosperity of the Promised Land, and nothing or no one could stop them from walking into their inheritance.

Are you determined to live your life as God designed? Are you ready to focus on your vision no matter how crazy it looks to you or others? Are you willing to move toward your promised land, even if you have to go by yourself?

Whatever you do, please do not waste valuable time and energy trying to get others to see what you see. They are not going to see what you see because God gave it for only you to see. Do not allow anyone to discourage or frustrate you because they are trying to see what you see against the backdrop of your past or current situation.

People will try to dissuade you with an array of pessimism; they will say things like, "that has never been done before," "you can't do it that way" or "that's not the way you're supposed to do it." You must immediately turn a deaf ear to their pessimism.

One of the main reasons you can have trouble advancing in your purpose is the loud conversation of a negative inner voice. Your negative inner voice will become an enemy to your future progress.

Your negative inner voice will repeatedly try to persuade you to believe lies about yourself. He or she will say things like, "You are not good enough," "No one's interested in listening to what you have to say," or "You don't deserve success." He or she will constantly sow these seeds of discord that can paralyze you into a perpetual state of stagnation.

I encourage you to move forward with your vision. Whatever God speaks into your life, you must believe, receive and achieve it. Caleb and Joshua understood that the people in the land were already defeated. They said in Numbers 14:9, "Only do not rebel against the LORD. And do not be afraid of the people of the land, because we will devour them. Their protection is gone, but the LORD is with us. Do not be afraid of them."

When you give into your fears and allow your vision to rot away, you are ultimately rebelling against God. You are saying, "God, I do not believe that you can fulfill your vision through me," or "God, you are not trustworthy enough to handle my situation." When you concede to this thought process, you discount His awesome power. This kind of false thinking allows your fears to take your eyes off your prize so that you miss your blessing.

The reason you are not advancing in life, or you keep losing the same battles, is because the enemy has duped you with his deceitful tricks and tactics. He loves to constantly bombard you with negative attacks that flood your mind with defeated thoughts. He shows you the struggles and hard work it will take to capture your prize. He brings people into your life who remind you of where you came from, what you did yesterday or how great your lack of resources is.

The enemy knows if your mind is preoccupied with negative thoughts you will not focus on your prize. He has devised a strategic plan to keep you from winning. He knows if you focus on your prize, then you can accomplish great things for God's glory.

So he comes at you with a ruthless and relentless attack to distract you with the seven poisons to your purpose. His motivation is to overwhelm you with a paralyzing fear that immobilizes you from going after your prize. He desires to fill you with:

1. **Desperation** – You do things contrary to the character God wants you to display.

2. **Defeat** – You feel like a failure so you do not pursue your vision.

3. **Diversions** – You become more attracted to the wrong things than the right things.

4. **Doubt** - You question God's vision for your life.

5. **Delays** – You put off doing what you know you need to do.

6. **Discouragement** - You focus on your problems rather than possible solutions.

7. **Disclaimers** – You talk against the purpose God desires for your life.

The enemy will use any number of these poisons to try to throw you off track. He wants you to give in to them so that you forfeit everything God envisions for your life.

I wrote this message to discredit the attacks from the enemy. I stand with you as Caleb and Joshua stood before Moses and the Children of Israel and declared they could possess the land, which God was leading them to. You can possess your land of promise if you keep your eyes fixed on your prize.

Like a track runner who wants to win her race, when the starting horn sounds, she takes off with her eyes focused on the finish line. She does not fix her eyes on the person next to or behind her. She knows if she focuses on anything other than the finish line, she stands a greater chance of losing.

You must possess the same concentrated mindset as the track runner. You cannot expend precious energy trying to run the race designed for another person. You cannot afford to waste valuable time looking over your shoulders to see who is coming. You must focus on running your race.

Let the enemy and all others know your eyes are locked in. Your heart is fixed. Your mind is made up. Your feet are progressing. Your hands are reaching forward to take hold of the prize God promised you and there is nothing anyone can say or do to stop you.

"Always focus on the front windshield and not the review mirror."
— Colin Powell

CHAPTER 19

YOUR CHARACTER MATTERS

"And His master saw that the Lord was with him and that the Lord
made all that he did to prosper in his hand."
— Genesis 39:3

Do you have the kind of character God can trust with His favor? In order to answer this question, you must first understand the definition of character.

Character is who you are when no one is looking and who you are when everyone is looking. In today's world, which is overly preoccupied with image, it is easy to worry too much about our reputation and too little about our character.

Building a reputation is largely a popularity venture, but building character requires you to focus on your values, actions and commitments. Noble talk and good intentions are not enough to build true character.

We can spend too much time trying to build our reputation so people will like us or speak highly of us. When we go out of the way to impress people, we can sometimes forfeit our character. Your reputation is what people think of you and your character is who you actually are! Reputations can change with your circumstances and can be inflated or destroyed in a brief moment, but Godly character is built through your daily walk.

God trusted Joseph with incredible favor because he knew Joseph's character would stand even under adverse circumstances. Joseph's character differentiated him from all the other servants in Potiphar's house. His impeccable character lead Potiphar to put everything he owned in Joseph's charge; and with Joseph there, he did not concern himself with anything except the food he ate (Genesis 39:6).

Potiphar knew he could trust Joseph not to steal, cheat or abuse his authority. Does your character communicate this kind of credibility? Does your character present a picture of respect, responsibility, care and fairness?

It is easy to display impeccable character when everything is going well or when everyone is patting you on the back telling you how awesome you are. But Godly character is disclosed by your everyday actions, including what you say and do when you think no one is looking or you think you can get away with something without being caught.

Reputations come and go, but character will hold you through the storms and pressures of life. If you spend your time and energy constantly building Godly character, you will never have to fear or be concerned about what others think or say about you.

Joseph's life represented a life built on solid Godly character. While Joseph was in Potiphar's house, when he was falsely accused of rape by Potiphar's wife, when he was thrown into prison and forgotten by the butler, his character never failed. Your true character is revealed by how you deal with the difficulties, pressures and temptations of life. When Potiphar's wife tempted Joseph to lie with her, he refused.

He could have easily allowed the pressure and temptations from her daily advancements to overtake him. He knew any action contrary to what he valued most would have been detrimental to his character and would have damaged his favor with God. He knew God still held him accountable to His character, even under this extreme pressure. He was so committed to living a life of Godly character that he told Potiphar's wife, "There is no one greater in this house than I, and he has withheld nothing from me except you, because you are his wife. How then could I do this great evil and sin against God?" (Genesis 39:9).

God is looking for men and women who have the character He can trust with His favor. Your ultimate focus should be living your life based on solid ethical values and principles. True Godly character requires you to surrender to God's direction, when it makes sense and when it doesn't. Men and women of character do the right thing even when doing right will cost them comfort. They understand the value of upholding their character is the key to progressing in God's vision for them.

Your character is revealed by your deeds and actions and not just words, especially when there is a gap between what you want to do and what you should do, or where you currently are and where you truly need to be. Maybe the reason you have not excelled in what God has purposed in your life is that your character is not in proper alignment.

It may be time to evaluate your character and see where you truly stand. Which type of person do you choose to be? The choice is yours.

Person without Character	**Person with Character**
Takes the easy route	Does the right thing
Controlled by feelings	Directed by values
Make excuses	Accepts responsibility
Gives up when challenged	Overcomes challenges
Seeks external motivation	Relies on internal motivation
Words & Actions Contradict	Words & actions agree
Choices lead to failure	Choices lead to success
Contrary attitude	Opens opportunities for others
Selfishness rules	Progressive attitude

"Be more concerned about your character than your reputation. Your character is what you really are, while your reputation is merely what others think you are."
—Dale Carnegie

CHAPTER 20

COURAGE IN YOUR PIT

"Then some Midianite traders passed by, so they pulled him up and lifted Joseph out of the pit and sold him to the Ishmaelites for twenty shekels of silver. Thus they brought Joseph into Egypt."
— Genesis 37:28

Do you have the courage to stand in your pit when faced with overwhelming circumstances? Have you ever encountered a pit situation that left you so fearful that you could not move?

What does it mean to have courage? Courage is standing when everyone else wants to run, speaking when everyone is afraid to speak, acting when everyone is paralyzed by fear, taking action in the face of danger, holding one's character and moral uprightness when everyone else is tempted to compromise theirs.

Every event in your life ordained by God will contribute to your overall vision. If Joseph's brothers had not schemed to throw him in the pit, or if the Midianites who took him to Egypt had been a day late, Joseph never would have been sold to Potiphar's house.

If Potiphar's wife had not lied about Joseph trying to rape her, he never would have been put in prison and he would never have met the chief butler who eventually recommended him to Pharaoh to interpret his dream. If this series of events had not happened, Joseph would never have been promoted to prime minister to save Egypt and his family.

Your life may have taken some strange twists and turns that you never dreamed would happen. You thought you were going on a smooth ride on a four-lane expressway to your dreams, but you ended up on a dark, bumpy, winding, endless dirt road to disaster. You did not plan on your life going in this direction.

You imagined that you would be making a great salary, living debt-free, happily married or owning your own business. You thought you would be living your American dream. But it seems that you are living the American nightmare. You are so far from where you dreamed you would be that you can't see any possible way for your dreams to happen.

God gave you a vivid picture of where you would be and what you would be doing, but He did not show you the pits that you would encounter. The reason He did not show you the pits is that you might have forfeited your future. You might have given up if you had seen the struggles. You might have remained in your comfortable situation because the challenges looked impossible to overcome.

God allows us to encounter different pits, without warning, to see if we really trust the vision He gave us. Will we walk away? He wants to know where our true worship lies. It is easy to worship Him when we are on the mountaintop and we have the support of others, but sometimes it becomes harder to worship Him when we are no longer on top and cannot find a person to lean on.

I admonish you to focus on your vision with more vigor while you are in your pit. When you truly worship Him, you are, in essence, saying, "I will live my life in total surrender to His will, whatever it may be." Your worship then becomes a lifestyle, not predicated on your current circumstances. You worship Him with the understanding that He will take care of you in or out of your pits.

You do not know when your deliverance is coming, but you know that He has the ability to deliver you at any moment. When you put your total trust in Him, you understand the pit is not your final destination. You know the one who ultimately holds your tomorrow is in control.

God wants to use you in your pit. That is the reason it is so important for you to stay connected to Him. During all of Joseph's pits, he remained connected to God. He realized that the pits were only temporary. He did not know how or when he would be delivered from them, but he determined to stay committed to the vision God revealed to him as a teenager (Genesis 37:5-19).

Every pit situation is an opportunity for you to show forth God's glory. You may ask, "How do you show forth His glory when you are dealing with a pit situation?" I say, "You submit to His will, stay true to yourself and follow His directions no matter what happens."

I learned in my most difficult pits that I must trust His leading. I admit I have tried, on several occasions, to handle the pit my way, and I blew it every time. When you view the pit with your own eyes, you feel inadequate, helpless, lonely and lost. It can make you feel like everyone is prospering and moving forward, but you are stuck and going nowhere. But, if you view your pits through God's eyes, you can come out restored, refined and regenerated.

I know many individuals who want to come out of their pits, but they are so locked in they cannot see a way out. They want to move from where they are, but they feel stuck. They want to have loving relationships, but they feel incapable. They want to live a progressive life, but they cannot find the motivation to move forward. They want to become productive and effective, but they cannot gather the momentum to change.

No matter what your pits may be, walk in courage, because God is able to give you victory. In the midst of his pits, Joseph knew he had one greater than him who would fight his battles. Just as Joseph weathered every pit through God's power and rose to live his purpose, you too can live the same example.

"Courage is the mastery of fear, not the absence of fear."
— Mark Twain

CHAPTER 21

CONSISTENCY PAYS OFF

"But the Lord was with Joseph and extended kindness to him and gave him favor in the sight of the chief jailer."
— *Genesis 39:22*

I remember watching a baseball game several years ago and the announcers were touting the shortstop from one of the teams as the next great shortstop. They were really hyping him up because he had made several spectacular plays in his very brief professional career. They were comparing him to several of the great shortstops in baseball history. That particular night, one of the greatest defensive shortstops to ever play the game was in the booth with the announcers.

The announcers asked him an array of questions about his career as a major league baseball player. They wanted to know the secrets that made him one of the greatest defensive shortstops of all time. He admitted to them that there were no secrets. He told them that it was his daily commitment to hard work and dedication to excellence that made him a great shortstop.

During their discussion, they brought up the fact that others had compared the new and exciting shortstop to him. They wanted to know his opinion about how this new shortstop compared to him. The great shortstop agreed that the young shortstop had great potential to be one of the best defensive shortstops in the game. He said he was still very young, though, and he would have to play several more years to deserve so much acclaim.

As they continued their discussion on the comparison of the young shortstop to the great shortstop, the comment stood out in my mind. He said the young shortstop must play the position at a high level of excellence day in and day out for many years.

The great shortstop played his position so consistently that he made the tough plays look routine. He performed at a high level of excellence that was not predicated on the score of the game or the team they played. I loved the way he ended the conversation that night by telling the announcers to call him in about ten years so that they could start making a real comparison.

The life of Joseph exemplified a life of consistency. Joseph suffered through some very difficult life situations. Through all of his difficult times, he remained very consistent in his walk with God. He knew God had a unique vision for his life and he did not allow his difficult circumstances to keep him from living it. While in the pit, he kept looking up. When delivered out of the pit into Potiphar's house, he quickly rose to the position of operations manager. Joseph's life was coming together until Potiphar's wife lied about him and he was thrown in prison.

Even in prison, Joseph's life was consistent with God's vision. He found favor with the warden and was put in charge of the prison. He was not in what many would consider an ideal situation. He was in prison serving time because of a lie. He was in a place that could have discouraged him from living his vision. He could have become consumed with why these things were happening to him. Instead, he decided that, since God continued to give him favor in adverse circumstances, he would live his life according to what he knew and believed.

You too can live a life aligned with God's vision even in unfavorable circumstances. You may ask, "How can I live consistent to my vision when everything seems inconsistent in my life?" I admonish you to keep doing what you know is right, and do it consistently every day. Keep praying and seeking His Word for directions. Keep listening to positive people who will encourage you to keep doing the right things. Keep encouraging yourself when no one else will. You will encounter situations that may hinder your progress, but you must remain consistent to living your vision.

Joseph vividly saw his vision, but his life was going in the opposite direction. He saw a day when his brothers would bow down to him. He saw a day when he would be the head and not the tail. He never envisioned being thrown into a pit by his brothers, working as a slave in an Egyptian house or being thrown in prison because of a lie. His dreams turned into what others would consider a nightmare, but Joseph remained consistent to his vision even when he did not understand the 'why.'

Joseph consistently stayed true to what he believed. I did not say he never felt frustrated or discouraged about his situations. I imagine sometimes he wanted to take matters in his own hands, but he fought off the temptation and did the right things. In the end, his consistent living placed him in a position of favor. When Pharaoh needed an interpreter of his vision, he called for Joseph. When he needed someone to manage Egypt's resources, he appointed Joseph.

If you are living inconsistent to your vision, it is not too late to get back into the game. Ask God to forgive you, and then repent (which is a 180-degree turn in your thinking that eventually leads you in the opposite direction of where you are currently going). It is never too late to break from your detrimental routine of inconsistency and start living consistent to your vision. In the end, the payoff and rewards are incredible.

"Consistency's path is straightforward and true; and its course, good or bad, helps you learn what to do."
— Wes Fessler

CHAPTER 22

COMMITMENT IS TESTED BY ACTION

"But he refused and said unto his master's wife. Behold with me here, my master does not concern himself with anything in the house and he has put all that he owns in my charge."
— Genesis 39:8

Have you ever made a commitment to yourself or someone and did not follow through? How did it make you feel?

How do you define commitment? It is a binding agreement between the heart, mind and emotions that moves an individual on a course of action towards his purpose. When you really commit to following what God purposed for your life, you will not allow the world's false promises deter you.

Commitment is not something that happens because you dream of it. It doesn't just show up because you say you want to accomplish a certain goal. It doesn't happen because you do a routine for a week or two. Commitment is tested by your daily actions and not your words.

If you have a job then you should commit to doing the very best you can while you are there. If you are married, you should commit to being a faithful and loving husband or wife. If you are a father or mother, you should commit to training your children in a Godly manner. If you want to grow in knowledge and wisdom, you must commit to being a lifelong learner.

In America, we have become a society of instant gratification. If things don't happen the way we want, we easily give up. If someone does not do things exactly the way we want him or her to do it, we will walk away. Many people are committed to something just as long as it is easy and beneficial to them. We forfeit some awesome blessings when we chose not to commit to our vision because things do not go our way.

Joseph is a great example of someone who represented the true definition of commitment. He made an unwavering commitment to follow his vision even under adverse circumstances. He was not going to let anyone or anything deter him from living his vision.

When Potiphar's wife made her moves on Joseph, he did not succumb to the intense pressure to satisfy his flesh. His commitment fortified him to resist her daily sexual advancements. He did not care how good she looked, how fine she was or that he might have gotten away with it. He knew God had entrusted him with an awesome vision and he was not going to give into her temptations or follow his flesh.

Potiphar's wife did not just give up because Joseph said, "I am not going to lie with you. She used his rejections as fuel for her burning desire to lie with him. She was not going to accept no for an answer. She kept coming after him day after day, but he did not yield to her advances. One day, she became very aggressive and grabbed him. I love what Joseph did next. Instead of giving into her aggression, he ran.

We need to follow Joseph's example, because the thing that is tempting us won't easily give up, either. When our commitment to our vision is being intensely pressured by temptations, we need to run. Sometimes merely trying to avoid temptation is not enough. You must turn and run, understanding that the temptation is far too great for you to stand against it.

Joseph understood a few moments of pleasure could wreck his future. His main concern was not that Potiphar would find out, but that he would be sinning against God. Joseph stood fast on his promise, but his refusal to lie with Potiphar's wife did not stop her advancements. It only intensified them. The scripture emphasizes that she pressured him day after day to lie with her, but Joseph kept singing the same song; "I cannot lie with you and forfeit my promise" (Genesis 39:10).

Isn't this just like the enemy? He loves to tempt you when you are most vulnerable. He waits until what he thinks is the right moment and comes at you full blast with his temptations of temporary pleasure. He thought he had Joseph in the right position. Joseph was far away from home, and he was a slave who was experiencing success. He may have even felt lonely. Therefore, the enemy used Potiphar's wife in an attempt to derail him.

You can make the same commitment Joseph made. Determine what is worth dying for and make that the basis for your decisions. Your vision is screaming for it. Those connected to you are counting on it. Your family is crying out for your unwavering commitment.

Because you commit to living your vision, do not automatically think everything is going to fall into place. Don't think everyone that is close to you will support your efforts. Don't think you are not going to encounter some struggles. Sometimes the exact opposite happens. Your life may get more chaotic. Things that once succeeded stop working. People, who said they would have your back leave you hanging. That does not mean you give up. It may mean you are on the right track to living out your commitments.

If you read the rest of Joseph's story, you will see all the benefits he reaped from committing to his vision. God eventually raised him from the prison to the palace. It may look scary and intimidating because you are about to make a commitment you have never made before. You are about to move from lip service to action, giving up to rising up, defeat to victory and ordinary to extraordinary. You may realize what you have been missing all this time is True Commitment.

"There's a difference between interest and commitment. When you're interested in doing something, you do it only when circumstances permit. When you're committed to something, you accept no excuses, only results."
— Unknown

CHAPTER 23

YOU CAN WIN YOUR BATTLES

*"Put on the full armor of God, so that you will be able to stand firm
against the schemes of the devil."*
— Ephesians 6:11

If you are like me, you may have tried to use your own tactics and weapons to fight your battles but quickly discovered the enemy's schemes and strategies were more deceptive than you first thought. You can live a life of victory in spite of the enemy's attacks against your vision. I know it is easier said than done. You are dealing with a present attack that is coming at you full steam ahead.

You don't want to hear another person tell you everything is going work out. You don't want to hear that this, too, will soon pass. You want real assurance and a guarantee you can really overcome the intense attacks against your vision.

To withstand every attack from the enemy, you must put on the whole armor of God. God is not going to put the armor on for you, nor is He going to make you use it. The choice is yours. If you make the choice to wear His whole armor, victory is possible. However, if you choose not to wear His armor and fight the battles in your own strength, you have just chosen spiritual defeat.

You can decide today to wear God's armor and put the enemy on the run. Fighting with His armor gives you an offensive attack that will release you from the enemy's dominion. Take a look at what will happen in your life when you wear the whole armor of God and use His weapons.

Gird your loins with the belt of truth. Girding your loins with the belt of truth holds your battle armor in place. The belt of truth empowers you to walk in integrity, holds your values and character intact, and equips you to diffuse the lies of the enemy. The enemy will tell you that God has left you, or that you will not make it or you will always be down and out.

If you are not wearing the belt of truth, your emotions can easily deceive you into living a life contrary to your designed vision. When you gird your loins with the belt of truth, the truth of your vision will come alive in your life, empowering you to victory over the enemy's attacks.

Put on the breastplate of righteousness. When you put on the breastplate of righteousness, you protect your heart from the fiery darts of the enemy. When your heart is protected, it keeps you in tune to God's direction for your life. You are constantly reminded to ask God to search your heart to make sure you are not harboring sin that will hinder you from living your vision in full effect. The breastplate helps filter your heart from the junk the world, the enemy, and other people feed you. Your heart is protected to love, lead and live the right way.

Shod your feet with the preparation of the Gospel of Peace. You wear shoes to protect your feet from injury when walking or running. You enjoy comfortable shoes because they give your feet the comfort they need to support your body's weight. In the same way, when you shod your feet with the preparation of the Gospel of Peace, you are prepared to stand in the comfort of His peace, even in the midst of the storms and pitfalls of life.

Take up the shield of faith. The shield of faith allows you to progress forward in your battles when the enemy aims and fires his arrows of evil. Picture yourself carrying the shield of faith in your left hand deflecting the fiery darts of fear, worry and doubt the enemy throws at you. When you are carrying your shield and advancing forward, it does not mean you have all the answers, but you have the assurance that God does. Pick up your shield and move in faith.

Wear the helmet of Salvation. Wearing the helmet of salvation protects your mind. The helmet protects you at all times in any battle because you are covered under Christ. You can claim the mind of Christ, which can stabilize your thoughts when the enemy is attacking your mind with his lies, rumors and deceit.

Use the Sword of the Spirit. You have the privilege to use the Sword of the Spirit, which is the Word of God, to wage an all-out assault against the enemy. You don't ever have to retreat with God's Word in your heart because it is readily available for instant use. The Word puts you on the offensive against every attack of the enemy. With the Sword of the Spirit at your disposal, you can advance in your vision and fulfill the promises in every area of your life.

Experience the Power of Prayer. Now that you are wearing the whole armor of God, you can progress forward in battle. It is God's desire that you progress forward in battle by seeking His face through prayer. It is through your prayers you come to know the direction for your life. It is when you pray that God speaks to you about your purpose (who you are), your vision (where you are going), your values (how you need to live) and your goals (what you need to do).

You can decide today to wear God's armor and put the enemy on the run. Fighting with God's armor gives you an offensive attack that will release you from the enemy's dominion and give you victory on the path to living your vision.

"The hero is the man who lets no obstacle prevent him from pursuing the values he has chosen."
—Andrew Bernstein

CHAPTER 24

HOW TO DEAL WITH THE PAST?

*"Brothers, I do not consider myself yet to have taken hold of it.
But one thing I do: Forgetting what is behind and straining toward
what is ahead."*
— Philippians 3:13

One of the ingredients necessary for an effective and productive life is to make sure you deal with the issues of your past. The truth is your past will continue to hinder you until you deal with it proactively. If you don't proactively deal with your past, it can affect your today in a negative manner.

In order to deal with your past, you **first must be honest with yourself**. We have a tendency to see the flaws in others (especially those who are close to us) and we will quickly point them out without hesitation. You may need to do what I did. Do an honest self-analysis, look in the mirror, and ask these questions: "Could my life be this way because of something in my past I have not dealt with? Have I been totally honest with myself and those who are close to me?"

We all bring baggage from our past into our relationships. We will quickly bring to the forefront the good things from our past because they produce the good qualities we want present in our lives. The bad things in our past, however, we have not dealt with; personality problems, emotional issues, relational difficulties and physical struggles create internal and external problems that can jeopardize our relationships.

The second thing to do is to surrender the issues to God and allow Him to reveal to you anything or anyone in your past you need to deal with. Whatever He reveals, do not procrastinate. Deal with it immediately and begin the process of moving forward.

The third critical issue is always forgiveness. We have all dealt with some kind of deep hurts from our pasts that still have negative influences over our lives. Without forgiveness, your hurts become festering wounds that never heal. An open wound can easily distract you from what is important: your sanity.

The simple act of forgiveness can set you free from your past and put you on the path to living a successful life. Please note simple does not imply easy. It takes a concentrated effort to forgive others and/ or yourself about past issues, but with God's help and a solid support system, you can do it.

Finally, you must take responsibility for dealing with your past. I want to let you in on a startling secret about the past: the past is the past and you cannot change it. Your past is like scrambled eggs. No matter how much you want to go back and change what happened, you can't. You want to blame someone, but you know passing the blame will not help your progress or change your situation.

Taking responsibility means acknowledging what happened and dealing with it in a responsible manner to bring about a positive resolution. If you regularly blame your spouse, your parents, your job, the government or others for what happened in the past and never take responsibility, you will never truly be set free.

If you waste valuable time thinking, "If I would've done it this way, I could've had this or I should've received that," stop that defeated thinking right now. I know you are not going to forget your past totally. You need your past to remind you of what not to do or what to do to focus your attention on your specific vision.

Your job is to be honest with yourself, surrender the past to God, seek forgiveness and take responsibility. Do not let the cynical words of others prevent you from chasing your dreams. Do not let fear or pride derail your progress. Do not let your past failures or mistakes abort your promised future. It will surprise you how quickly your life and relationships will begin to change for the better when you deal with your past.

"One problem with gazing too frequently into the past is that we may turn around to find the future has run out on us."
— Michael Cibenko

CHAPTER 25

DEFINE YOUR VALUES

"If it be so, our God whom we serve is able to deliver us from the furnace of blazing fire and He will deliver us out of your hand, O king. But even if He does not, let it be known to you, O king, that we are not going to serve your gods or worship the golden image that you have set up."
— Daniel 3: 17-18

The three Hebrews boys (Shadrach, Meshach and Abednego) are great examples of what it means to live your core values. Even under extreme pressure from the king to worship his idol god, living their core values was non-negotiable. The Hebrew boys were so committed to living their core values that when the king threatened to throw them in the fiery furnace because they would not bow to his idol, they did not give in. They did not know whether they would be delivered from the fiery furnace or not, but without wavering they did not back down on what they valued.

What would you have done in this situation? Would you have bowed to the king's idol or would you have remained faithful to your core values? The three Hebrew boys chose to remain faithful to their core values. Their core values became the filter through which they determined right from wrong, significant from insignificant and purpose from pleasing people. Even though following their core values could have potentially cost them their lives, they would not deny the God they believed and trusted.

The king eventually had them thrown into the fiery furnace. This fiery furnace was not a small conventional oven for cooking your dinner. It was a huge industrial furnace that could have been used for baking bricks or melting metals. The king was so enraged by the Hebrew boys that he had the furnace turned up seven times hotter than normal. "He answered by giving orders to heat the furnace seven times more than it was usually heated" (Daniel 3:19). The temperatures were hot enough to ensure no one could survive the heat.

Your fiery furnace may be the pressures of your job, the persistent attacks against your marriage, the problems with training today's children or the perpetual lack of money in your bank account. Just as God rescued the three Hebrew boys, He is able to deliver you from your fiery furnace. When He delivers you, you will come out unharmed by the fire (Daniel 3:27).

The Hebrew boys stood on what they valued, and God rescued them from what looked like certain death in the fiery furnace. I believe the greatest blessing was not their deliverance from the fiery furnace, but their willingness to die for what they valued the most.

They could have easily made excuses and bowed to the king's idol in order to save their lives. They could have said, "We will bow down but not actually worship the idol;" or "Everyone else is bowing to it;" or "We will do it this one time and God will forgive us." But, instead of making excuses, they put their faith in action.

To become effective in your life's journey you need to identify and develop clear and concise core values. Your core values are central to defining who you are, what you do and where you are going. Once defined, they should guide you in every aspect of your life. When you make a conscious decision to follow your core values, you will not let anyone or anything persuade you to live against them. It is these core values that determine what is important to you as an individual.

The surprising thing is that if you ask most people what their core values are, many could not give you a solid answer. Some would give you a list of values, but they would not be able to prioritize them. They will give you a list that sounds spiritual, but they don't come close to living them. In order to live the vision that God has designed for you effectively, you must develop a set of prioritized core values that guide your daily life. Your core values should be

1. **Clearly Stated** – You should have a set of clearly written and prioritized core values that guides your daily life.

2. **Conscientiously Chosen** – Your core values should be in direct agreement with your God-given purpose.

3. **Continually Executed** – You should make a solid commitment to live your values daily no matter what is currently happening in your life.

4. **Consistently Followed** – You are responsible for consistently living your core values.

5. **Constantly Evaluated** – You should constantly evaluate your values to make sure you don't need to reprioritize them, make any changes or adjustments.

You may ask, "How do I determine my core values?" **First**, you need to define what core values are. Core values are deeply-held beliefs that define what is right and fundamentally important to each of us. They provide guidelines for your daily choices and actions. **Second**, to determine your values, start with what God's Word says we should value. "But the fruit of the Spirit is love, joy, peace, patience, kindness, goodness, faithfulness, gentleness, self-control; against such things there is no law" (Galatians 5: 22-23). **Third**, to determine your core values, you need to pay attention to your life's experiences, prayer responses, family up-bringing and personal preferences.

Once you establish your core values and start living them watch your life begin to turn in a different direction. Do not get frustrated and quit if it seems difficult, but keep praying, believing and living through the process.

"Strive for integrity - that means knowing your values in life and behaving in a way that is consistent with these values."
— Unknown

CHAPTER 26

STICKS AND STONES

"Death and life are in the power of the tongue and those who love it
will eat its fruit."
— Proverbs 18:21

You have probably heard the old saying, "Sticks and stones may break your bones, but words will never hurt you." Wrong! It's because words have such a powerful effect that we devise defenses against them. If words truly did not matter, we wouldn't put as much emphasis on the power of words. The Bible says, "Life and death is in the power of the tongue" (Proverbs 18:21).

James puts incredible emphasis on the power of the tongue by saying, "So also the tongue is a small part of the body, and yet it boasts of great things. See how great a forest is set aflame by such a small fire!" (James 3:5).

Negative words can cause more damage than a stick or stone breaking a bone. A broken bone will heal within a few months, but a damaging word can cause pain for a lifetime. Think about the young man who is continually told he is like his sorry, no-good father or he is not smart enough. After hearing these damaging words day after day, year after year, he begins to believe them. When he grows up, he becomes a living testimony of the very words spoken over his life.

Think about the young woman who is constantly told she is ugly and no man would ever want her. Hearing these negative words infiltrates her thinking and results in her believing the lie. She begins to give herself over to any man who approaches her with enticing words. Her self-esteem and confidence are deflated because of the degrading words spoken into her life. I can give story after story of the devastating effect negative spoken words can have on a person's life.

One of my favorite stories that illustrate the power of the spoken word is in my favorite movie, "The Five Heartbeats." In a scene early in the movie, Eddie King, Jr. was talking to his father about his singing aspirations.

During their conversation, Eddie's father made what I thought was a very damaging statement. Eddie told his father of his desire to become a famous singer, and his father commented by saying something to the effect of, "I wasn't nothing, so you will never be nothing." He used more seasoned words than I used, but you get the point.

In the movie, Eddie became the famous lead singer of The Five Heartbeats. The fame and fortune would soon become Eddie's Achilles' heel and would eventually cause him to venture down the wrong road. He went down the dark, unforgiving road of alcohol and drug abuse. He forfeited his fame, fortune and family for perceived pleasures. I believe the power of his father's words had a drastic impact on Eddie King's outcome.

I know that this is a movie played by actors, but in real life, there are millions of individuals living defeated lives because of the damage of negative spoken words. They have allowed the negative words to keep them in a perpetual hostage mentality. They have believed the detrimental lies of the enemy and thus live life void of God's vision. Negative spoken words from the enemy and others can keep you and God's vision for your life locked in a sealed, lonely box, never allowing you to experience the awesome blessings on the outside.

What if we decide to season our talk with positive and encouraging words? What if we decide to permanently close our ears to others' negative and pessimistic spoken words, and tune into what God says about who we are and what we can do? What if we stop believing the curse words of the enemy and start believing the elevating Word of

God? I suggest that you read God's Word for empowerment, listen to inspiring messages and surround yourself with people who encourage and challenge you to achieve better.

At the end of the Five Heartbeats, Eddie King was restored. One of the former group members, Choirboy, told him that God could change his life. Choirboy took it upon himself to go after his friend. He knew God could take a shattered life that was in a million pieces and put it back together again, better than ever.

At the end of the movie, we see Eddie singing in the church choir, his family back together. He was overcoming his alcohol and drug addictions. The power of encouragement can do wonders in the life of an individual. Eddie King, Jr. went from the bottom of the world to the top, to the valley and to restoration.

I definitely know sticks and stones will break your bones, but I believe the power of encouraging and empowering words can change your life. When our spoken words are seasoned with God's life-changing Word, we will see self-esteem rise, the suicide rate plummet, discouragement transformed to encouragement, peace of mind overshadow depression and defeat turned into victory.

"Think twice before you speak, because your words and influence will plant the seed of either success or failure in the mind of another."
— Napoleon Hill

CHAPTER 27

LISTEN TO THE BUMBLEBEE

*David said to Saul, "Let no man's heart fail on account of him; your
servant will go and fight with this Philistine."*
— I Samuel 17:32

Did you know scientists once thought the bumblebee should not be able to fly? Did you know that the bumblebee did not listen to the doubters or naysayers?

Scientists' beliefs were based on its size, weight and body shape in relation to the total wingspan: a flying bumblebee is scientifically impossible. The bumblebee, ignorant of scientific input, decided to fly anyway.

Like the bumblebee, you and I can't afford to let the negative words of others and the cynical reports from the media deter you from going after your dreams. Turn a deaf ear to the pessimistic words spoken by discouraged and discontented people. Ignore the stings of negative input and discouraging thoughts and replace them with positive input and empowering thoughts. If you do, you will position yourself to achieve things no one else thinks is possible!

What I truly love about the bumblebee is his motivation to accomplish his purpose, in spite of what scientists and others once believed. What truly motivates you? Do you have a written vision plan that motivates you to live a life of excellence in your family, marriage, health, career, business, finances and spiritual life?

There are thousands of people who have great goals and well-thought-out plans but who never achieve anything of significance. They lack the motivation to make their vision a reality. You and I need the kind of motivation I read about in an article by Randy Slechta. "Motivation supplies you with the courage to look at yourself in the mirror and realize that you can achieve more than you have," he says. "It drives you to be better than you ever have before, propelling you to great heights of success."

When you are motivated to achieve your vision, you will develop and implement powerful vision goals that motivate you, no matter what the cost. Real motivation from within provides you with the internal fortitude to tackle any obstacles in your path.

David, the young shepherd boy, defied the odds to challenge the giant who was terrifying the army of Israel. His inner motivation drove him to refuse to accept things the way they were. He could not stand by and let Goliath disrespect God and His people.

He could not walk away and let Goliath win. Something had to be done. Someone had to step up to the plate and take on the challenge from Goliath. David's motivation did not come from the men of Israel, because they were too busy hiding in fear. His brothers didn't motivate him; they were too consumed with criticizing and finding fault in him (I Samuel 17:28). Saul did not motivate him, because he was too absorbed with telling David he was too young to go against the champion warrior (I Samuel 17:33).

David was prepared for this moment. Goliath was a threat to his people, his future kingdom and his promised kingship.

He was so confident of victory that when the giant approached him, instead of backing down in fear, he ran toward him with only a sling and five smooth stones. I Samuel 17:48 says, "Then it happened when the Philistine rose and came and drew near to meet David, that David ran quickly toward the battle line to meet the Philistine."

Is your current place in life where you desire to be? If not, what are you going to do about it? Are you willing to do things differently and defeat the giants in your life with the tools God gave you?

You need to focus more intensely on where you desire to be and begin to make all the necessary changes to get there.

- You can't wait for the right person to show up in your corner to cheer you on.
- You can't wait for the right season to get ready.
- You can't wait for something magical to happen to motivate you to move.

Your eagerness to motivate yourself to move comes when your desires meet your God given purpose.

Neither the bumblebee nor David let what others said was impossible stop them from achieving what they knew was possible. The bumblebee did not wait to get the approval from scientists. David did not wait to get advanced military training.

The bumblebee did not spend years studying how to fly. He launched out and flew. David did not wait forty more days to study a manual or take a class on how to fight giants. He stepped out in faith and believed God for victory. The bumblebee and David went against the odds and did the inconceivable. Are you ready to do the same?

"Nobody can make you feel inferior without your consent."
— Eleanor Roosevelt

CHAPTER 28

SEE YOUR FUTURE

"Now the Lord said to Abram Go forth from your country, and from your relatives and from your father's house to the land which I will show you."
— *Genesis 12:1*

Do you believe God designed an incredible future for you? Do you possess the faith to focus on your future when your situation does not match what you believe?

God has designed an incredible future for you. He desires for you to have a successful vision that will impact the future of every area of your life. When God begins to unfold your vision for your future, you will need to have the faith to walk it out daily. Your life progress depends on it. Your family is relying on it. Individuals you do not know will be blessed by it.

You must see the promise of your future even though your present situation is totally opposite of where you need and desire to be. You may ask, "How can I accomplish this?" You accomplish it by keeping your focus on your promised future and blocking out all of the unnecessary distractions.

Abraham is one of the most fascinating characters in the Bible; a man God entrusted with an extraordinary future promise. He took an ordinary man who had no hope of having children and made him a father of a nation of people. God's promise to Abraham looked impossible from the human intellect, but with God all things are possible. He worked in and through Abraham's life to give him a future that blessed generations.

Abram (his name before God changed it to Abraham) was 75 years old when God called him to depart from Haran on a promise. Abram was instructed to leave his family and everything he was accustomed to and go to a new land God would lead him to.

The move he and his family were about to make required him to move in faith toward the vision God revealed to him of a greater future. He did not fully comprehend where God was leading him. He did not know the exact location of the land. He didn't know who or what was on the horizon. The only thing he knew was that God made him an incredible promise and he was going to take Him up on it. "So Abram departed as the Lord had spoken to him," (Genesis 12:4).

Abraham's faith for a brighter future fueled his vision. Without faith in this vision, there would have been no great nation. His vision would have died in Haran. He had to believe that a nation was coming from him, even though he didn't have any children. "But Sarai was barren, she had no child," (Genesis 11:30).

He had to trust God that the promised child would come from Sarah, even though she was well passed the birthing age. God changed her name to Sarah from Sarai to emphasize that she would be a mother of nations. Abraham decided to believe God and move toward his promised future that would bless generations after him. He believed, not because he could see how things would turn out or because he could see the land with his physical eyes. He believed because the God of all creation made him a promise.

Open your ears, mind and heart to the sound of your vision. It may be a faint sound smothered by life's circumstances, but it's still playing. Your past mistakes may resurface to drown out your future progress, but the beat of your vision is still heard in the background.

People may tell you what you can and what you should do, but you tell them you are following the sound of your vision. You must have faith that the future God promised you will come to pass, in spite of everything happening around you. You can start today by taking the necessary steps to prepare you and your family for your promised future.

Make a commitment today to see your promised future fulfilled. Even through the difficulty and hardships of life, you must see the greater possibilities that lie ahead. Once you place your future in God's hand, everything you need to live it out will eventually fall into place. You do not have to live a life full of anxiety and fear. You do not have to exhaust yourself worrying about what others might think or say. Your future is in God's hands. If you can see your promised future according to His plan, success is definitely possible.

God promised to bless Abraham and make him great, but there was one condition: he had to obey His directions. This meant he had to leave his home, friends and family to travel to a new land that was only a promise. Abraham obeyed, walking away from everything he knew for a promise that he couldn't physically see or grasp. God may require you to leave possessions, positions, places and people of comfort and stretch your faith. Please don't let the comfort and security of your present position make you miss your promised future.

It is time to see your future as God does. Do not look at your future through the lens of others or your own finite thinking, because you will limit the power of God operating through your vision. Do not look at your future through the lens of your current situation or circumstances, because they are only temporary. You must view your future through the lens of God's Word. When you look at your future through the lens of God's Word, the impossible becomes possible. The unreachable becomes reachable. The conquered becomes the conqueror. See your future and live as God sees and watch your vision come to pass.

"I have a dream that one day on the red hills of Georgia the sons of former slaves and the sons of former slave owners will be able to sit down together at the table of brotherhood... I have a dream."
— Martin Luther King Jr., "I Have a Dream"

CHAPTER 29

THINKING FOR A CHANGE

"For as he thinks within himself, so he is..."
— *Proverbs 23:7*

Has your negative thinking kept you from moving forward in your vision? Does negative thinking keep reminding you of the failures and mistakes of yesterday? Negative thinking can convince you that you can't live an effective life because you have been in a negative situation for too long. Negative thinking can make you feel like you can't be successful, you can't do anything right, and you can't live past yesterday's problems, today's circumstances or tomorrow's challenges.

You cannot afford to let negative, stinking-thinking cause you to live life below what you are capable of living. God's purpose and vision for you to live will not only change your life but will help change the lives of those connected to you.

Several years ago, I read a powerful inspirational story about Roger Bannister. Roger Bannister was the first runner to break the four-minute mile. Before he broke the record, it was widely believed to be impossible for a human to run a mile in under four minutes. It was believed the four-minute mile was a physical barrier that could not be broken because of the significant damage it could cause to a runner's health. The barrier of a four-minute mile seemed impossible to break.

On a spring day, May 6, 1954, Roger Bannister did what others thought was impossible; he crossed the finish line with a time of

3 minutes and 59.4 seconds and broke what others thought was an impossible record.

The barrier that no one thought could be broken physically turned out to be something bigger-- a psychological barrier that could not be broken in the mind. Until Roger Bannister decided to break through the mental barriers, he could have never achieved the incredible record-setting feat.

So what happened to the physical barrier that had stifled runners for years from breaking the four-minute-mile? Was there a sudden transformation in the human make up? No! Did Roger receive some kind of super power that enhanced his ability? No! It was the change in thinking that propelled Roger to break what others thought was an insurmountable record.

When he broke through his four-minute psychological barrier, it released hundreds of male runners to break through their negative mindsets and realize that it was possible for them to achieve the same. I believe the same can be true in your life; that when you break the barriers in your own thinking, it leads to others breaking the barriers in their own thinking.

What artificial barriers have you placed in your life? What negative, inner-conversations have you been speaking to yourself? Have you told yourself that you are not smart enough to get the promotion, or that you don't have enough experience to start the business? Have you succumbed to thoughts that tell you constantly you don't deserve a better life, or that you will never make enough money to live debt free? Have you convinced yourself with your own negativity that achieving your vision is impossible or out of your reach? Have you literally talked yourself out of going after what God specifically promised you?

If you convinced yourself of this, today is the day to change your thinking. If God promised that you can achieve beyond your current situation, then it is possible. Your responsibility is to trust what God promised you, believe it and go after it. You may have to go it alone. You may have to let go of some people or give up some possessions. You may have to stay up late and get up early. The only way you are going to obtain victory is to keep thinking forward.

I imagine Roger Bannister heard an earful of negative and discouraging talk. He heard the media say breaking the four-minute-mile was inconceivable. He heard the doctor's reports that said it is beyond human possibility. He heard the analysts say the record would never be broken. At times, he may have said, "What am I doing? Maybe this record is impossible." But, Roger decided to fight through the obstacles, shut down the negative inner conversation and accept the challenge.

Roger's hunger and drive deep within kept pushing him to his ultimate goal of breaking the four-minute-mile. His powerful vision of breaking the record would not allow him to quit or give in to the naysayers. His mind was made up and his will could not be broken. When he broke through his psychological barriers, the once impossible record became possible. No negative reports. No discouraging opinions. No false barriers could stop him from achieving what he knew was attainable.

The best step you can take to pursue your vision is to change how you think. If Roger Bannister had accepted that the four-minute mile was impossible, he never would have attempted to break through his mental barrier. He would have allowed the negativity to dissuade him. He would have complied with the naysayers' voices. He would have consented to the dream-killing experts. Instead, he decided to go after his dream.

Just think of all the things in your life God has shown you are possible. If He said it then you can believe He can bring it to pass through you. However, Roger Bannister not only believed he could break the four-minute mile record; he exercised his belief. To finally breakthrough your four-minute mile you must believe the impossible and in the famous words of Nike®, "Just do it®."

Watch your thoughts, for they become words.
Watch your words, for they become actions.
Watch your actions, for they become habits.
Watch your habits, for they become character.
Watch your character, for it becomes your destiny.
— Author Unknown

CHAPTER 30

IT IS IMPORTANT TO HAVE A DREAM

"Then Joseph had a dream, and when he told it to his brothers,
they hated him even more."
— Genesis 37:5

I am not referring to the dreams you have while sleeping. I am not referring to dreaming of winning the fifty-million dollar lottery or signing to play pro-basketball for ten-million a year. I am talking about a dream that God has placed in your life that is connected to who you are and where you want to go. You could also call them aspirations, goals, plans, visions or desires.

Do you have a dream that is so big you have no hope of accomplishing it apart from God's help? It keeps you up at night. You think about it constantly. You know if you don't go for it, you will miss living your best life.

God desires to fill our hearts with big dreams. He desires for us to live a maximum life that glorifies Him and blesses others. I have been guilty of dismissing big dreams because it seemed impossible at the time. I canceled the dream before I started because of doubt and fear. I made the mistake of thinking that the dream was about me making it happen instead of waiting to see God work through me.

Two people who have really encouraged me about the importance of having a big dream are Joseph in the book of Genesis and Martin Luther King, Jr., the great civil rights leader. They both exemplified what is possible when you have a big dream that you take action on no matter what is going on around you. Their dreams provided the glue that motivated them to focus on achieving the impossible.

Your dreams will do the same in your life if you act on them. They will give you a purpose for your everyday activities. They will push you to progress forward when life's circumstances try to push you backward.

In Joseph's life, he experienced many ups and downs that are recorded in Genesis, chapters 39-48. He could have easily given up on his dream that God revealed to him at seventeen. God showed him that his brothers and father would, one day, bow to him.

When he told his brothers, it enraged them with so much hatred that they threw him in an empty pit. Joseph did not allow the pit to dissuade him from his vision. While in the pit, Joseph kept his eyes focused on his dream. Do you have the heart and mind to focus on your dreams even when your current situation stinks?

If you read the rest of the story, you will see that Joseph's dreams were fulfilled at the end. Don't give up on your dreams. You may have to step back and recalibrate your directions. You may have to go by yourself. You may have to endure difficult trials, but a dream of a better future should motivate you to focus forward in spite of any difficulties.

Dr. King had a powerful dream that influenced a movement; that changed the face of an entire race and nation. Though he was criticized, beaten, jailed, house-bombed, threatened, ridiculed and ostracized, he kept his dream alive. His dream was so inspirational and impactful that, after more than forty-eight years, it still resonates in the hearts and minds of those who hear it. The dream still prompts people to take action.

In his famous "I Have a Dream" speech, delivered on August 28, 1963 from the steps of the Lincoln Memorial, you can hear the intensity his dream for a better future commanded.

"I say to you today, my friends, so even though we face the difficulties of today and tomorrow, I still have a dream. It is a dream deeply rooted in the American dream.
I have a dream that one day this nation will rise up and live out the true meaning of its creed: 'We hold these truths to be self-evident: that all men are created equal.'
I have a dream that one day on the red hills of Georgia the sons of former slaves and the sons of former slave owners will be able to sit down together at the table of brotherhood.
I have a dream that one day even the state of Mississippi, a state sweltering with the heat of injustice, sweltering with the heat of oppression, will be transformed into an oasis of freedom and justice.
I have a dream that my four little children will one day live in a nation where they will not be judged by the color of their skin but by the content of their character.
I have a dream today."

As I write about two of the greatest dreamers that ever lived, I am reminded that God gives each of us a dream that He wants us to fulfill. He is not going to do it for us. It is up to us to live our dreams. If we do not, the dreams will die with us and the world will miss our contribution. In anticipation of living my dreams, I have realized **Seven Keys to activate your dreams**:

1. Spend quality, uninterrupted time seeking God's face.

2. Make sure your dreams are in line with your core values.

3. Never downplay your dreams, no matter how big or small.

4. Make your dreams strong and vivid so that they engage and empower you to achieve them.

5. Write them down in detail and post them in a visible place where you can see them every day.

6. Think about them daily – make sure your daily activities are in line with actually living your dreams!

7. Review your dreams periodically to see where you are in the process.

Having a dream from God is very powerful. It's important to note this dreaming process only works when it's carried out through daily action. To dream is the start. To live the dream is the payoff.

"Every great dream begins with a dreamer. Always remember, you have within you the strength, the patience, and the passion to reach for the stars to change the world."
— Harriet Tubman

CHAPTER 31

GOALS MATTER!

"Then I said to them, "You see the bad situation we are in, that Jerusalem is desolate and its gates burned by fire. Come; let us rebuild the wall of Jerusalem so that we will no longer be a reproach."
— Nehemiah 2: 17

What is a Goal? A goal is an aim, a purpose or a sense of direction toward which you move all of your energies, desires and efforts. Goals are the targets toward which you point your life.

Goal setting is an extremely powerful tool for accomplishing your life's vision. If you ask most people what their goals and plans for their life or families are, many would not be able to give you specifics. Some would give vague and unrealistic answers and say things like, "I want to be wealthy"; "I want to do God's will"; or "I want to own a business." They will give general answers that are not goals, but are dreams desired by many people.

People fail to achieve their goals because they attempt to live life without a real plan. Imagine a football coach trying to lead a football team without a game plan, a builder trying to build a house without a blueprint, or a CEO trying to lead a business without a business plan. All of the examples above perpetuate confusion because the leaders are trying to operate without a plan.

You must have clear and specific goals that give your life direction. Without clear goals, you can end up going around and around in circles living an unproductive and unsatisfied life.

- Have you sought God for your goals?

- Have you written down your goals?

- Do you have a plan on how you are going to get to where you want to go?

- Have you determined the benefits you and others will enjoy by achieving your goals?

- Have you identified the obstacles to your goals?

- Do you know what resources, skills or people you might need?

- Have you set realistic dates for accomplishing your goals?

- Do you have a progressive attitude that pushes you toward your desired goals?

Until you seriously answer these important questions, you really do not have goals; you may have a set of stagnant dreams.

Goals are not written in concrete or unchangeable terms, but they do give you a starting point and a destination to reach. I am not promising a magical formula that provides a guarantee your goals will automatically happen if you read this material or attend some expert's seminar. Nor am I suggesting that if you follow our twelve steps you will have no struggles and everything will happen in your life the way you want at the exact time you desire. In order to achieve your goals, you must make sacrifices, commit daily, overcome challenges and work your plan. No one can do it for you. It is your responsibility. Your life has greater meaning when you are working toward the goals you desire.

Once you have a goals plan - now what? Many people agree on the positive impact that a goal-setting plan can have. Many individuals have used goal-planning sheets to list their major goals, but that is where they stopped. They defined their goals, but never implemented the plan.

Are you going to act differently and implement a plan to succeed in achieving your goals? The key word here is **ACT**. Take immediate action on your plan! Do not procrastinate! Do not wait for the right moment! Time is slipping away and your deadline is inching closer with each passing second.

Do something each and every day toward the accomplishment of your goals. Work with passion and energy on the first step of your plan until it is either completed or until you can make no further progress on it. Then move to the next step, coming back to those incomplete steps as soon as you can move them forward to their completion. Keep moving! Keep working! Keep taking action steps every day! Do not stop!

Anyone who has ever started an exercise program will tell you the hardest part is getting started. That first week or two can be tough. You are sore and your body hurts in every place, but if you can get through that initial beginning period, then the process becomes easier.

Once you have been actively involved in your exercise routine, it will still take effort, but it takes far less effort than if you stop for a few weeks and try to start your routine all over again. Taking consistent daily action will not only move you quickly toward your goal, but it will reinforce in your subconscious mind that it is possible to achieve your goals.

Here is a picture of someone with goals and without goals. Which type of person do you believe God desires for you to be? Which do you choose to be? The choice is yours!

Person without Goals	Person with Goals
No real direction	Sense of direction
No real excitement in living	Excitement about life
Accepts average	Pursues excellence
Critical of others who are successful	Appreciates others who are successful
Lacks purpose & positive values	Strong sense of purpose, values & worth
Settles for living an unproductive life	Seeks a creative, effective & active life
Poor steward of time, resources & energy	Seeks a balanced & focused life

The time is now for you to go after your goals. It is time for you to awaken the dreams that live inside of you. It is time for you to create a goals plan that focuses on multiple areas of your life. Success is not just professional and financial, but relational, physical, spiritual, mental and social are equally important areas of achievement. All of these make the whole, balanced person. This is the whole person concept of Goals Matter!

Your written goals plan will help you to see where you are going, what changes you need to make and if you are progressing toward the prize that is set before you. It is time to stop: making excuses, putting off today for tomorrow, wasting valuable time and energy and missing out on what God designed for your life.

"What you get by achieving your goals is not as important as what you become by achieving your goals."
—Zig Ziglar

CHAPTER 32

PURSUE YOUR GOALS

"...came up behind Him and touched the fringe of His cloak, and immediately her hemorrhage stopped."
—Luke 8:44

Are your daily actions bringing you closer to your goals? If not, do not expect the things in your life that you need and want changed to change. It feels comforting to hear motivational speakers tell you how to achieve the goals to make your life prosperous.

It is very inspiring to read books and articles on how to overcome the challenges in life to fulfill your desired goals. All of these are great for encouraging and empowering you to set and pursue your goals. However, the key to achieving any goal is putting feet to your faith.

I do not care how many conferences, seminars and faith services you attend, you must do your part. I do not care how many more classes or studies you participate in, you must take action. If what you are doing today is not getting you any closer to where you desire to be, stop fooling yourself. You are going to have to make some adjustments and changes and start doing things differently for the results you desire.

If you are like many people, you want to change, but find it hard to follow through. You have faith for a moment, but after a while, your faith dissipates. You get excited and are ready to go, but somewhere in your process, you are met with an obstacle or challenge that shuts down your pursuit. You lose your commitment, and your confidence turns to uncertainty. After a while, you allow things to go back to the way they were. You allow your physical sight to dissuade you from pursuing your promised future.

One of my favorite inspiring stories of an individual pursuing and accomplishing a goal is the Bible story of the woman with the issue of blood. This story is rich with inspiration and revelation on what happens when you make up your mind to pursue your goals even in the face of certain barriers.

It is encouraging to see someone, despite her current circumstances, commit to accomplishing a desired goal. Her goal of being healed gave her something concrete to focus on and that focus had a positive impact on her actions. She knew exactly what she wanted, how to get it and she had the unction to go after it.

I am greatly motivated and inspired by this woman's courage and perseverance. She had a focused vision that would not allow anyone, or even her current issues, to stop her. Her vision for healing drove her to move in total faith.

She decided to stop wishing and waiting and move in unshakable faith to receive her healing. I believe her healing was already present before she touched the hem of Jesus' garment. Her healing was waiting to manifest in her life when she actually got up and moved toward what she believed was possible.

Here are three important truths that we can extrapolate from this woman's pursuit of her goal.

1. **She had to do something she had never done before.** This woman had spent the last twelve years of her life trying everything she knew to be healed. She had visited every doctor and specialist in the city and they could not heal her. She had taken all the medicine prescribed for her continual bleeding, but they could not cure her issue.

   She had exhausted all her financial resources, but still could not get a breakthrough. She finally concluded that the only way she was going to experience her healing was to do things differently. She had done the same things year after year, but instead of getting better, she grew worse.

After years of growing worse, she finally decided her previous actions kept leading her to a dead end road. She remembered hearing about the healings of Jesus. She heard about people who were blind, lame or sick that were miraculously healed by Jesus. She decided to make a life changing decision to think, speak and act differently. She said, "If I only touch His garment, I will get well." What she decided to do was totally different from what she had ever done before.

What do you need to do differently in your life to pursue your goals? What area(s) in your life do you need to simply walk by faith and not by sight? What rewards are waiting for you when you step out in faith?

2. **She seized her moment.** She knew Jesus was on the scene. The healing she had been seeking for twelve long years was at her fingertips. This was her moment. This was her opportunity to get to Jesus, the only One who could heal her issues. She knew this moment might never come again. She did not care who was in the crowd. She didn't care what others had to say.

She knew this was her moment to break free of twelve long years of isolation and desolation. She put all anxiety and fear under her feet and walked on them in faith. She put guilt and shame in her back pocket and bent down to touch the hem of his garment.

There are moments in life when you have to overcome fear and just exercise your faith. You must come to the point when you say, "I am tired of living a life less than what God has destined me to live." You must say with confidence, "Though I don't see how, where or when my vision will manifest itself, I am determined to pursue it with a tenacious faith."

When your moment comes, you can't wait for others' approval. You can't wait to see who is going to go with you. You can't wait for things in your life to be perfect. You must seize your moment at the time it comes because you may never get that same opportunity again.

3. **She opened doors for others.** When she touched his garment, there was something different about her touch that distinguished her from everyone who was touching Jesus. Her touch was from a heart of real unconditional faith.

   She did not come for any games or gimmicks. She did not come for the applause of men. She did not come to make friends in the crowd. She came to receive her healing. She came for restoration. Her touch was so powerful that Jesus said, "Somebody touched me for I perceived power going out from me." (Luke 8:46). Even though the crowd was pressing him on every side, He knew this woman's touch was pure. Her touch was from a heart of faith.

God desires for you, in the twenty-first century, to have a walk of faith that is as real as this woman's. When you walk in this kind of faith, you will see issues healed in your family, community, city, church, nation, government, business and world. But it will only come from a faith anchored in God's directions.

When the woman realized that Jesus knew it was her, she had to come forward. She had to go public with her testimony. Her testimony was a powerful encouragement and blessing to all those who were present in the crowd. Her act of courage opened the door for others to see unprecedented faith in action.

Do not think your story is insignificant. If God made a way for you out of what looked like an impossible situation, share your testimony. If He saved your life from the pit of hell, share your story of deliverance. If He brought you out of depression, share your story of hope. If He brought you from death to life, share your story of restoration. Whatever He has brought you out of, share your story so others can see and experience the powerful presence of God.

God is looking for individuals who are ready to break free from traditionalism and stagnant habitual routines and glorify Him through the pursuit of their goals. He is looking for individuals who are ready to move from dreaming to doing, from talking to walking, from complaining to conquering. When you pursue your goals with unwavering faith, watch the doors of opportunity open before your eyes.

"Time is free, but it's priceless. You can't own it,
but you can use it. You can't keep
it, but you can spend it. Once you've lost it you
can never get it back."
–Harvey MacKay

CHAPTER 33

BELIEVE YOU CAN SUCCEED

"I can do all things through Christ who strengthens me."
—Philippians 4:13

What do you believe makes an individual successful? How do you define success? If you ask ten individuals their definition of success, you probably will get ten different definitions. Success does not look the same for everyone because the picture of success is different for every person.

A basketball coach might define success as winning a championship. A CEO might define success as leading the number one company in his or her industry. An employee for a manufacturer might define success as a promotion to a management position. A father might define success as training responsible young men. You can see from the above examples success is defined differently depending on the individual.

Success is possible for everyone. It is not distinguished for a select group of individuals. It is not based on your family background or what side of the tracks you come from. Real success is more than the accumulation of money, the acquisition of material possessions or the amount of personal achievements.

To have real success, you must have a continuing desire to become the person God destined you to be. Success then becomes a daily process. Earlier in my life, I defined success differently than I do now. At first, I thought success was making a great salary, driving a nice car, living in a nice home and working in a marketing position for a major company.

Do not get me wrong: there is nothing wrong with having any of these as a part of your success journey, but they should not define what true success is. If your success only consists of these things, then you have a very limited definition of success.

Dr. Charles Stanley in his book, "Success God's Way," states that "… our human approach to success tends to be 'Here's my goal.' God's approach is 'Here's the person I want you to be, here's what I want you to do and here's how to be that type of person and how to do your given task.' It is being a godly person and then obeying God in His directives that we find success."

When I began to listen to God's direction, my thinking on success changed. I saw there were things more important than just money, possessions, positions and personal achievement. I realized my relationship with God, my wife, children, family and others were more important to my success than the material things. I also discovered my character, values, health, integrity and thoughts were a very important part of my success journey. In my search for true success I discovered a new definition.

Success is becoming the person God purposed you to be, living positive values that guide your daily choices and actions, accomplishing the goals that give your life direction and sowing seeds that empower others.

The Apostle Paul understood what it meant to live a successful life. Paul was so committed to living for Christ that even in times of lack or prosperity, times of want or satisfaction, he learned to be content (Philippians 4:12). Not the type of contentment that allowed him to settle for where he was, but a type of contentment that reassured him God would give him success despite His current circumstances.

Paul knew how to live successfully because he saw life from God's point of view. He focused on his assignment and not on what he thought he should do or what others were doing. He detached himself from the nonessential things and focused on the things of value to his ultimate destiny. He was not trying to imitate Peter, John or any other Apostle. He determined in his mind he would succeed by becoming the best man God designed him to be.

You cannot rely on your strength because you have weaknesses and insecurities. You cannot rely on the strength of others because they are dealing with their own pains and problems. You cannot rely on the strength of the economy because it is unstable and unforgiving. You cannot afford to rely on the strength of a job, because you may have a job Monday morning, but by lunch, you may be unemployed.

None of these are reliable because they cannot give you the solid foundation you need to support your promised future. However, when you place your future in God's hands, you have the firm foundation you need to put your vision on the right road to success.

God wants you to succeed and stands ready to help you beyond what you can ever dream or think. Paul said it best in Ephesians 3:20: "Now unto Him who is able to do far more abundantly beyond all that we ask or think, according to the power that works within us."

"The price of success is hard work, dedication to the job at hand and the determination that whether we win or lose, we have applied the best of ourselves to the task at hand."
— Vince Lombardi

CHAPTER 34

HOW TO GROW YOUR POTENTIAL FOR SUCCESS

"This book of the law shall not depart from your mouth, but you shall meditate on it day and night, so that you may be careful to do according to all that is written in it; for then you will make your way prosperous, and then you will have success..."
— Joshua 1:8

Living successfully is a life-long journey, full of trials and triumphs, ups and downs, the good and the bad; but most of all, it is one big learning experience. When you realize that you are not the only person who goes through tough circumstances or bad situations, things become clearer. At some point in life, everyone experiences negative situations, and that should help you to know you are not alone.

Achieving success is largely about how you respond to those negative situations, and how well you pick yourself back up and continue with living your vision. It is your vision, and nobody else is going to do it for you. It is up to you to seek God for directions on how to live your vision the right way. When He reveals your vision, you must fight through everything to achieve it.

God created you in His image. He created you with a unique purpose, and it is up to you to realize what your purpose is so that you can spend your lifetime working to fulfill it. Once you understand your purpose, your vision will become clearer.

How do you find out what your purpose in life is? You ask God. Only the creator of a thing can tell you what the function of that thing is.

You are unique. Do not let anyone tell you otherwise.

It is your responsibility to grow your potential for success so that you stand out to the world and shine the way God designed you to shine. Success is not just going to show up at your front door in a nicely wrapped package for you to receive it. It is not going to be handed to you on a silver platter with all the trimmings. It will take some effort and time to achieve the success you desire. Even if you have no idea of what you need to do, you can start by focusing on how to grow your potential for success.

Here are four key principles to apply to your life that will put you on the right road to growing your potential for success.

1. Focus on one main goal.
Reaching your potential for success requires you to focus on one main goal at a time. You may have other goals, but you should have an overarching goal in each of the areas of life (spiritual, relational, physical, financial, social, mental and professional) that is your main focus.

You cannot accomplish a goal if you are scattered in twenty different directions. You must decide where to focus your attention and what you are willing to give up to make your goal happen.

What main goal can you set in each area of your life to focus on?

2. Focus on continual improvement.
Every day you should do something that makes you better than you were yesterday. The only way to reach the success God desires for your life is for you to make a commitment to continually improve each day.

Never think that you have arrived. You can always improve. You can always learn something new. You can always grow. You will find that what you get as you continue to improve daily is not as important as what you become along the way.

What can you commit to doing daily that will improve your life?

3. Forget the past.

I have learned in life that you cannot move forward if you are dragging the past behind you. If you focus on the past how can you possibly see your future? Your past can be a boat anchor to your future progress.

I understand you won't totally forget your past because it is a part of your life, but you do not have to allow it to dictate who you can become and where you are going. Do not let past mistakes, failures or success prevent you from reaching your future potential for success. Today is your day to officially let go of the past and grab hold of your promised future.

What past mistakes, failures or successes do you need to leave in the past so you can move forward?

4. Focus on the future.

It is God's desire for you to have a successful future that will have a positive effect in every area of your life. Your potential for a great future lies ahead of you. It is paramount you live your present in such a way that it ignites your future possibilities.

Paul said it best in Philippians 3:13-14; "Brethren, I do not regard myself as having laid hold of it yet; but one thing I do forgetting what lies behind and reaching forward to what lies ahead. I press on toward the goal for the prize of the upward call of God in Christ Jesus."

When you focus on your future there is no way you can keep your eyes and mind stuck in the rear view mirror of yesterday. If you do, you will miss living the future you were destined to live.

What steps do you need to take today to focus on your future?

"Success is not final, failure is not fatal: it is the courage to continue that counts."
— Winston Churchill

CHAPTER 35

FIVE KEYS TO SMART GOAL SETTING

"Trust in the LORD with all your heart and do not lean
on your own understanding.
In all your ways acknowledge Him and He will make
your paths straight."
— Proverbs 3:5-6

Do you want to make your dreams a reality? Are you ready to get past just talking about your dreams and start making them happen?

If you are like most people, they talk and dream about achieving their goals. At the beginning of each year, millions of people create a wish list of things they want to accomplish. We usually call this list our New Year's Resolutions.

I was one of the many people who set New Year's Resolutions, but before the end of January, I had either given up, fallen behind, reverted back to things as usual, overdone it or failed. The real tragedy is not that I failed at achieving my resolutions, but rather I didn't have a specific plan to implement to position me for success.

Planning is an essential part of setting specific vision goals. No successful business, corporation or organization was built without a plan. You may have great dreams and high expectations, but without a plan to implement, they are just lofty aspirations.

Every year I developed a list of good intentions, but I had no real plan in place on how to accomplish my goals. Therefore, every year I was left with a feeling of failure, discouragement and disappointment, because I never came close to achieving my desired goals.

Your goals will not automatically happen because you write them down and pray. You must work to make your goals happen. You will make some mistakes. You may even fail at achieving some of your goals. Through every discouragement and disappointment, you must maintain a positive outlook that you can make your goals a reality.

The key to achieving your goals may require you to change how you think and the way you do things. The main key to success is developing some simple easy-to-follow guidelines. There is no magic or special formula. You must work smart. You must exercise your faith.

I want to equip and empower you with a unique way of looking at the **SMART** way to set goals. **SMART** is the acronym for five qualities of setting a goal. Our **SMART** method will equip you with a solid guideline to define your target and the inspiration to go after it.

1. **Specific** – One of the most important qualities of an effective goal is that it is specific. When your goals are specific, you know exactly where you want to go and what you need to accomplish. There is no confusion and doubt because the more specific you make your goal the more focused you become. A specific goal does not take you around in circles, but it puts you on the right road to your destination.

   An example of a specific goal to set is, "I am going to lose 20 pounds." I wrote the goal in a positive and affirmative manner. I did not say I might or I think.

2. **Measurable** – Goals have value only if you establish concrete criteria for measuring progress toward attaining each goal you set. When you measure your goals, you make them quantifiable. You see your target dates and you experience the excitement of seeing your progress. If your goals are not measured, it will make it tough for you to stay motivated to complete them when you have no milestones to indicate your progress.

   An example of a measurable goal is losing 20 pounds within the next four months. You establish a begin date of March 1, 2013 and a target completion date for July 6, 2013.

3. **Actionable** – Successful people not only set goals, they take action. They do not spend a whole lot of time talking and wishing about their goals. They develop a goals plan, and then spend the bulk of their time executing their plan.

    What good is it to have great written goals plan and never act upon it? You can talk about how much faith you have to believe that your goals can come true, but until you put feet to your faith, your goals will remain stagnant dreams. The secret to achieving your goals is to get started.

    In our example of losing 20 pounds, you may need to develop an exercise routine that starts out fifteen or twenty minutes every other day. Start with deliberate action and begin to work your way up. You may have to begin cutting back on certain fatty foods and replace them with healthier foods. If you will stick to your plan as much as possible, you will find these small actionable steps will pay off.

4. **Reinforcing** - When you set actionable goals, make sure they are in agreement with your values. You should not set any goal that does not support your core values. Your core values are your fundamental beliefs that provide guidelines for your daily choices and actions. Any goal outside of your core values will take you away from your vision course.

    It does not matter how good the goal looks, how much potential money you can make or how popular it will make you. If your goal does not reinforce your core values, stay away from it.

    In our weight loss example, let's say one of your core values is to be in good physical health. Our goal of losing 20 pounds in four months would be a great goal to reinforce your core values.

5. **Trackable** – Now that you have made your goals specific, measurable, actionable and reinforcing, you need to create a plan to track them. I have said it before and I will reiterate again: your goals are not written in concrete.

   As you take action on your goals, you will need to continually track your progress in case you need to make any adjustments or changes. You may find some goals you track do not really contribute to your overall vision and need to be eliminated.

   The goal of losing 20 pounds by July 6, 2013 is easily tracked using our Goals Matter! Planning Sheet. Our goals sheet will help you stay on target and let you know if you need to make any changes to your plan.

"It must be borne in mind that the tragedy of life does not lie in not reaching your goal. The tragedy of life lies in having no goal to reach."
— *Benjamin E. Mays*

CHAPTER 36

12 SIMPLE STEPS TO ACHIEVING YOUR GOALS! STEPS 1-3

"Then I said to them, 'You see the bad situation we are in, that Jerusalem is desolate and its gates burned by fire. Come; let us rebuild the wall of Jerusalem so that we will no longer be a reproach."
— Nehemiah 2: 17

No one can easily talk you out of accomplishing a goal worth pursuing. It is a goal that rests deep within you, and you cannot let it go. Your focus becomes so intense on achieving your goal that you will not allow current circumstances, and what others say, hinder you. You will focus on your goals with laser beam attention because you understand that accomplishing them is part of you becoming the person God desires.

Nehemiah developed a consuming desire to accomplish his goal of rebuilding the walls of Jerusalem. He felt such deep compassion that he wept and mourned for days when he heard that God's people lived in distress because of the broken down walls in Jerusalem. He sought God in prayer for direction on what he needed to do. He prayed as a man of action, not a sideline critic. He does not pray, "God give this goal to someone else," or "God you need to do something about this issue." Instead, his prayer is, "God use me to make something happen," (Nehemiah 1:4-11).

When you commit to your vision and express it in achievable goals, you provide yourself with the motivation of where you are going and how you anticipate getting there.

Are you passionate about achieving your goals? Nehemiah's passionate and uncompromising heart to go after the goal God gave him positioned him for success. He did not allow anyone or anything to compromise his focused goal of rebuilding Jerusalem's broken down walls. My desire is to help you develop and implement a solid goals plan that will help bring your vision into fruition.

Our Twelve Simple Steps to Achieving Your Goals will help you write and implement an achievable goals plan. We will take a practical look from the Book of Nehemiah on how to set and achieve your desired goals.

1. **Spend quality time seeking God for your goals**. Before Nehemiah started rebuilding the walls of Jerusalem, he spent four months in prayer seeking God's directions. He committed to spending the quality time needed to hear what and how to proceed with his goal and whom he would need to ask for help. He prayed, "Let your ear now be attentive and your eyes open to hear the prayer of your servant..." (Nehemiah 1:6).

   I advise you to get alone in a quiet place by yourself, away from the distractions of life, and begin to seek God's face. Put away your mobile devices, shut down the computer and turn off the television. Tell your family and friends this is your set time for seeking God's directions and you do not want to be disturbed. Do you have a daily appointment with God to seek Him for your life's direction?

2. **Define your goals in writing**. I believe during Nehemiah's four months of praying to God about rebuilding the walls of Jerusalem, he developed a detailed written goals plan. His goals plan helped him clarify what he needed from the king and the steps he needed to take to put his plan into action. "And a letter to Asaph, the keeper of the king's forest, that he may give me

timber to make beams for the gates of the fortress for the wall of the city…And the king granted them" (Nehemiah 2:8).

It is very important you take your Bible, pen, paper and a Goals Matter! Planning Sheet with you during your quiet time. When you begin to define your goals in writing, make sure they are SMART: Specific – Measurable – Actionable – Reinforcing – Trackable. Record in detail what God reveals to you, because you are fooling yourself if you think you can remember everything He tells you.

We tend to forget things. Write down your goals! Written goals bring clarity to your life. Written goals focus your attention. Documenting your goals in writing creates a road map to focus your directions. You will begin to see clearly what you need to do and how you need to do it.

3. **Create measures for success.** Now that you have defined your goals, the next step is to create ways to measure your progress. Nehemiah defined his goal and set a targeted time with the king on his return. "Then the king said to me, the queen sitting beside him, 'How long will your journey be, and when will you return?' So it pleased the king to send me, and I gave him a definite time" (Nehemiah 2:6).

It is not enough to say I have a goal; you need to have a way to measure your progress. You define your measures for success by:

1. Term (length of time)
   (a) Short Term (within a year)
   (b) Medium Term (within three years)
   (c) Long Term (over three years)
2. The Life Area – spiritual, relational, physical, social, financial, mental or professional.
3. Dates – Start date, target completion date and actual completion date.

Adding these measurables to your goals brings a greater energy and excitement to achieve them. If you don't meet your measurable, please don't give up. You may need to make some readjustments or changes. You may need to quit doing something one way and try doing it another way.

"Delight yourself in the Lord; and He will give you the desires of your heart. Commit your way to the Lord, trust also in Him, and He will do it."
—Psalms 37: 4-5

CHAPTER 37

12 SIMPLE STEPS TO ACHIEVING YOUR GOALS! STEPS 4-7

"What are these feeble Jews doing? Are they going to restore it for themselves? Can they offer sacrifices? Can they finish in a day? Can they revive the stones from the dusty rubble even the burned ones?"
— *Nehemiah 4:2*

4. **Define possible opportunities for success.** One of the keys to staying motivated while achieving your goals is to define your opportunities for success. Nehemiah knew rebuilding the walls would put the children of Israel in a more stable condition. The walls represented power, protection and peace for the city of Jerusalem and the people who lived there.

The walls were desperately needed to provide protection for the people and the Temple from the enemy's attack. Without the rebuilt walls, the city would remain defenseless against its enemies. Nehemiah was committed and consumed with accomplishing this goal because he understood the awesome opportunities that were possible once the wall were rebuilt.

One technique that I found very helpful to focus my goals planning was to list several opportunities for success in accomplishing a particular goal. I personally like to list three to four opportunities. Let's use the example of a goal of losing 20 pounds in four months.

Here are a few things I would list as possible opportunities for success: I will physically feel better, I will be more confident, I will have to buy a new wardrobe and I will have the energy to participate in more physical activities. You can list as many opportunities for success as you desire. Your list will become a huge part of your motivation to achieve your goals when times of discontentment, discouragement and doubt show up.

5. **Identify obstacles to success.** Now that you have spent time seeking God for your goals, you have written them down, set measures to success and defined possible opportunities for success, everything should be smooth sailing, right? Wrong! Obstacles will come to attempt to detour your goals. You will be able to identify some of the obstacles in the beginning, but some will come out of nowhere.

As soon as Nehemiah and the people began to rebuild the wall, the opposition came. "Now it came about that when Sanballat heard that we were rebuilding the wall, he became furious and very angry and mocked the Jews. What are these feeble Jews doing? Can they finish in a day?" (Nehemiah 4:1-3).

You may feel fearful about going after your goals because you know that opposition will come. You may think your life will be easier if you stay in your comfort zone, but opposition will come whether you stay in your comfort zone or not. Therefore, you might as well do what you need to do to accomplish your goals.

When you are growing and moving toward your goals, God equips and empowers you to deal with any obstacles. Nehemiah overcame his opposition by remaining focused on his main goal of rebuilding the walls. He didn't allow the naysayers and doubters to stop him from pursuing his goal. He identified the obstacles, prayed and kept moving forward.

I suggest you identify at least three obstacles that you feel may try to prevent you from achieving your goals. List the potential obstacles that you have identified for each of your goals on your Goals Matter! Planning Sheet and begin your journey of overcoming them to successfully achieve your goals.

6. **Breakdown goals into manageable action steps.** Nehemiah understood that rebuilding Jerusalem's broken walls would be a big project. He knew in order to achieve this goal he had to break down the larger goal of rebuilding the walls into smaller manageable action steps. One of the first things he did when he arrived in Jerusalem was to go out at night to survey the totality of the project.

After carefully studying the severity of the broken down walls and the burned gates, Nehemiah developed a comprehensive action plan. His approach was to divide the work of rebuilding the walls into forty sections. Then he would assign the appropriate people to each section. Breaking down the larger goal into more manageable sections would make the job easier to monitor and complete (Nehemiah 2:11-16).

When you have a large goal you want to accomplish, the best thing to do is break your large goal into smaller, more manageable action steps. If you focus on the enormity of the large goal, it can become too overwhelming. If you try to do the large goal all at once, it can lead to certain frustration and quick burn out.

If you take the large goal and break it down into smaller measureable action steps, you set yourself up for success, because you make your large goal more obtainable. It is much easier to bust a large stone with several small strikes than one big hit.

If you have a large goal you want to accomplish, our Goals Matter! Planning Sheets have a section where you can list at least ten smaller steps with a begin date, target completion date and an actual completion date. Taking the time to break your goal into smaller manageable steps will put you on the right road to your goals success.

7. **Identify people, resources or skills needed.** Nehemiah asked the king for specific resources that he would need in his wall-rebuilding project. He asked the king for letters to give to the governors for passage through their provinces (Nehemiah 2:7-8). He also asked for a letter to give to Asaph, the keeper of the king's forest, so that he would supply them with the timber they would need to rebuild the walls and his house. Nehemiah plainly identified what he would need in order to bring his vision to pass.

Not only did he identify the resources he would need, he also identified the people he would need to make this vision happen. Nehemiah knew he couldn't carry out this big vision alone; he would need to solicit the help of the entire Jewish community. He didn't go to a select group, but he involved everyone in the wall-rebuilding project. He requested the help of the priest, nobles, officials and others from the community (Nehemiah 2:17-18).

What resources or skills do you have or need to acquire to accomplish your goals? Who are the people you will need on your team to help you achieve your goals? You may have to take a class or do an in-depth self-study on a particular subject to educate yourself on a new skill or re-educate yourself on an old skill you will need. Trust me; you are going to need help from others.

Don't be ashamed or too prideful to ask for help. You can't do it alone. You will need support, encouragement and someone to share ideas with. Identify and acquire the resources, skills and/or people you will need and go to work.

"There is no short cut to achievement. Life requires thorough preparation - veneer isn't worth anything."
—George Washington Carver

CHAPTER 38

12 SIMPLE STEPS TO ACHIEVING YOUR GOALS! STEPS 8-12

"So the wall was completed on the twenty-fifth of the
month Elul, in fifty-two days."
—Nehemiah 6:13

8. **Demonstrate a progressive attitude.** Nehemiah was continuously confronted with opposition as he moved forward in rebuilding the walls of Jerusalem. At every turn, he was constantly threatened. Nehemiah, however, combated every threat with prayer and a progressive attitude to continue to move forward. His enemies said, "They will not know or see until we come among them, kill them and put a stop to their work" (Nehemiah 4:11).

Nehemiah did not back down. He stationed men behind the wall and people in families with swords, spears and bows (Nehemiah 4:13). He constantly reminded the workers of their ultimate goal by encouraging them to not be afraid of their enemies, but remember the Lord who is great and awesome, and He will give them victory.

The things that occupy your thought life can have a tremendous influence on your attitude. What you think and say will play an integral part in your ability to achieve your life goals. You must have a progressive attitude that moves you forward in spite of the opposition and barriers that are present.

How you think will determine who you are and what you do. Whatever you feed your mind will eventually come out in your talk and actions. When you catch yourself thinking defeated thoughts or speaking negative words, immediately replace them with positive words and empowering thoughts.

If you do not, your defeated thoughts and negative words will over shadow any attempt to display a positive and progressive attitude. The best way to get your thoughts in order is to align them with God's Word.

9. **Take action.** Nehemiah didn't just talk or wish about accomplishing his goal. He took action throughout the entire process. When he heard about the broken down walls of Jerusalem, he prayed to God. Next, he asked the king for his help and resources, he surveyed the walls and devised a plan, he organized the people to rebuild the walls, he stood up to those who were against the goal and they rebuilt the walls in record time.

What actions have you taken to turn your goals into reality? Once you have a written goals plan, it is time to take action. It is your responsibility to make daily decisions to do something to move forward. You can't wait for the right deal, the right people to support you or the right situation to happen before you take action on your goals. You could have written the most captivating, compelling and challenging goal possible, but if you don't take a course of action to implement your plan, your goal will remain just a wonderful dream. Once you have a desired goal, you can use our Goals Matter! Planning Sheets to properly set your goal in detail, and then take immediate action.

10. **Monitor your goals regularly.** I believe Nehemiah monitored the progress of the wall-rebuilding project daily. He probably had the leaders of each section give him daily reports of their progress and the actions of their opposition. Nehemiah kept a hand on the heartbeat of rebuilding the walls to make sure they were progressing in the right direction toward its completion.

As you move forward with your goals, you will need to periodically monitor them. It is important to know where you stand in your goals progress in order to make any necessary adjustments or changes. You may find that you need to go right instead of left, or you may have to extend the time required to complete an action step or the overall goal.

You may discover that a goal you set needs eliminating because it no longer aligns with your overall life's vision. Monitoring your goals regularly gives you a view of where you are and whether or not you are on the right course to completing your goal. Our Goals Matter! Planning Sheets are great documents to regularly monitor where you are on your goals progress.

11. **Reward yourself.** During Jerusalem's wall rebuilding project, there were many things that were accomplished. The people learned to work together as a team, they were able to overcome intense opposition, they learned about the power of prayer and they stopped oppressing their own people. All of these were great rewards for coming together as a team to accomplish a common goal. I believe their greatest reward came when they completed rebuilding the walls in a record time of fifty-two days (Nehemiah 6:15).

I don't want to make achieving your goals all work. You have heard the saying, "all work and no play makes you dull." During the process of reaching your goals, you need to implement rewards that follow key steps in your action plan. This will enforce your desire to move forward to the next step on your way to accomplishing your big goal.

Please make your goal achievement a fun and exciting process. Don't overdo it with rewards because you still have an overall goal to reach. Your minor victories deserve applause! You can establish bigger rewards as you accomplish more steps to your overall larger goal. This recognition will enforce where you are going and provides an incentive to get the job done.

12. **Keep moving forward.** Nehemiah committed himself to re-building the broken down walls of Jerusalem. Nothing or no one was going to stop him. He kept the vision moving forward in spite of opposition from people who didn't want to see the walls rebuilt (Nehemiah 4:1-3). He kept moving forward when they were threatened with death if they continued rebuilding the walls (Nehemiah 4:11-12). He kept the vision in front of them when internal schisms, inequalities and injustices could have derailed them (Nehemiah 5:1-13).

Throughout the impossible goal, Nehemiah displayed an uncanny ability to overcome obstacles and opposition to stay focused on his ultimate goal. Because he kept moving forward, the walls of Jerusalem were rebuilt in record time, and he brought about a spiritual awakening among the people of Judah. Nehemiah gives three motivators to help you keep moving forward in your goals progress.

a. Commit to your specific goals path regardless of setbacks, challenges or failures.

b. Continually surround yourself with people who will encourage your forward movement.

c. Consistently show up every day to do the work necessary to achieve your goals.

d. Confidently operate in your abilities, talents and gifts.

e. Courageously fight through the temptation to quit.

"Success comes from knowing that you did your best to become the best that you are capable of becoming."
—John Wooden

CHAPTER 39

STIR UP YOUR GIFT

"Wherefore I put thee in remembrance that thou stir up the gift of
God, which is in thee..."
—II Timothy 1:6

Recently I read a story about Louis Armstrong, the great jazz artist. Armstrong reportedly applied to go to music school when he was a young man. It is told that at his audition, he was given scales to sing, but he could sing only the first two notes properly. After his audition, the judges told him he didn't have what it took to be a musician. The story said that he cried at first because of the rejection from the music school.

He did not allow the rejection to hinder his dream of becoming a jazz artist. He told some friends, "I know there is music in me and they can't keep it out." If you know your music history, then you know Louis Armstrong became one of the most successful and beloved jazz musicians of all time. He sold more records and made more money than many other jazz musicians who were more talented than he was. Now Louis Armstrong is forever etched in the history of music.

What made the difference for Armstrong? The difference was that he knew his gift and he did not allow what others had to say to keep him from going after his dream. He knew that there was music in him and he was going to get it out. He determined in his mind he wasn't going to waste valuable time feeling sorry for himself. Instead, he put his energy into developing his gift of music. When he put in the time and energy to stir up his gift, the world opened its doors to receive his gift.

What is your music? Are you ready to play it to the fullest? You can experience success in your life just as Louis Armstrong when you go ahead and play the music that is inside of you. It will position you to become the person God has designed you to be. You will live life with a different step.

Your success does not depend on the state of the economy, what careers are currently in demand, or the state of the job market. Do not allow a perceived lack of resources or what people think you can or cannot do to hinder your progress. The principles found in scripture will enable you to stir up your gift and fulfill your vision no matter who you are or what your background may be.

Here are **twenty-one insights** to encourage, equip and empower you to stir up your gifts.

1. Your gift will make room for you in the world and enable you to live your unique vision.

2. If you believe you are too old or too young to use your gift, you believe a lie.

3. When you realize and develop your gift, it will equip you to live your vision with power.

4. It is your responsibility to STIR UP YOUR GIFT!

5. You stir up your gift by developing, refining, enhancing and using it.

6. You are the sum total of the choices and decisions you make every day.

7. You can choose to stay where you are right now, or you can choose to move forward in life by pursuing your God-given vision.

8. Challenge yourself to stop making excuses for why you cannot accomplish what you were born to do. Take your life out of neutral.

9. Most people do things because they have to. Wouldn't you like to do things because you have decided to base them upon your gifts?

10. You must choose to be on the offensive rather than the defensive.

11. You were created to stand out and not to blend in.

12. You were born with the potential to live an extraordinary life.

13. You were created to accomplish something that no one else can accomplish.

14. Never expect anything less than the highest thing you can go after.

15. Don't let people tell you, "You shouldn't have high expectations." Always expect more than what you have and what you are currently doing.

16. No matter how challenging life gets, don't give up, because your vision is the key to fulfilling your life's purpose.

17. Your gifts will initiate a passion in you to pursue God's vision for your life at all costs.

18. Your gifts are the primary motivator of human action and, therefore, will empower you to fulfill your vision.

19. Your gifts will influence the way you conduct your entire life.

20. Your gifts will expand your thinking, increase your sight and elevate your walk.

21. God created your gifts for you to use, but if you don't use them, you and the world will miss out.

"Do not go where the path may lead, instead go where there is no path and leave a trail."
—Ralph Waldo Emerson

CHAPTER 40

WORK YOUR PLAN

"But prove yourselves doers of the Word and not merely
hearers who delude themselves."
—James 1:22

Now that you have written your purpose statement, listed your core values, set your goals and described your future, it is time to work your vision plan. It is great to have a well-written plan that you and others can see and reference, but it does you no good to have a well-written plan and not work it.

The plan God gives you is the plan He desires for you to activate. You cannot afford to sit back and wait and think that God is going to hand you a free ride to living your vision. You must go to work.

In working your vision plan, you will encounter challenges and obstacles that will try to make you quit. They will come at you daily with negative thoughts and words of failure, but you must remain focused on your plan. Paul said it best: "I press on toward the goal for the prize of the upward call of God in Christ Jesus" (Philippians 3:14).

Paul had a vision plan to get to his ultimate goal and he wasn't going to let anyone or anything stop him. He pressed forward. When people are telling you it is not going to happen, you have to keep pressing. When you are telling yourself you are not going to make it, you have to keep pushing forward. When you are tired and defeat looks imminent, you must keep fighting.

You can pretend God's vision for your life will simply manifest itself with a couple of prayers, hearing an inspiring sermon or attending an empowerment seminar. It will not happen. You must roll up your sleeves, put on your hard hat and go to work to fulfill your vision.

Whatever God calls you to do, remember that He gave you everything you need to get the work done! He provides whatever resources, finances and people you need to help put your plans into action. God will not work through you if you are not willing. He gives you a choice and He will not make you do anything. If you are disobedient, you risk losing the blessings and abundance that come through obedience. If you are not willing to work your plan, you cannot get mad or upset if He uses someone else who is willing and obedient to carry out the plan you should have been working.

You must tirelessly stand against the temptations that will try to settle you in a comfort zone. You must fight to overcome the intense desires to procrastinate. You cannot afford to let laziness and slothfulness infiltrate your life. You have a vision to work.

The enemy wants to keep you complacent, fearful and doubtful. He does not want you to even try to live your vision. He will give you a good job; a wonderful position, a large salary, a nice bank account and prized possessions that will make you feel important. They masquerade as the real thing, but in reality, they can become the very things that keep you from living your intended vision.

The vision God gives you may not match up with your current situation. You may think living the values God prioritizes in your life seems impossible. The goals that God gives you may be more than you believe you can handle. The future that God shows you may look ridiculous compared to where you currently are. You may still think there is no way your vision can happen. You must remind yourself over and over, day after day, that if you keep working God's plan, then your vision can become a reality.

"Whatever course you decide upon, there is always someone to tell you that you are wrong. There are always difficulties arising, which tempt you to believe that your critics are right. To map out a course of action and follow it to an end requires courage."
—Ralph Waldo Emerson

CHAPTER 41

NO MORE COMFORTABLE PAIN

"When Jesus saw him lying there, and knew that he had already been a long time in that condition..."
—John 5:6

Are you missing your potential possibilities because you have become comfortable with where you are? Are you stuck in your comfort zone?

What is a comfort zone? Tony Jeary gives a great definition of a comfort zone. "It is a mental state in which you lose the momentum to pursue a vision because you have accepted where you are as the best you need to be or do." Do you continue to complain and grumble about your situation while doing nothing about it? It is easy to find yourself in situations that you really hate but have become comfortable in.

You know you need to do things differently, but you allow familiarity to keep you living in a comfortable pain. You know you need to make a move. You are unsatisfied with where you are and it seems as if life is rapidly passing you by. Your job is sucking the life out of you, but you stay where you are, miserable and unhappy, because you say, "I have to pay the bills or there are no jobs out there." I am not suggesting that you quit your job, but I am saying that you can proceed to look at other opportunities and develop an action plan to pursue something different.

You may know that there is a business in you, but you are intimidated to step out because you do not know if you will succeed. I am of the opinion that it is better to fail trying to do something than to stay where you are living in a comfortable pain.

I read a story a couple years ago that really hit home. A man was visiting a friend, and as he was approaching the porch, he could hear his friend's dog moaning and groaning. When his friend answered the door he asked him what was wrong with the dog. His friend said, "He is lying on a nail." This baffled the man because he wondered why the dog would continue to lie on the nail when it was obviously causing him pain. He asked his friend, "Why doesn't the dog just get up?" His friend said, "I guess it doesn't hurt badly enough."

When I read that story, the first thing I said was, "That dog was crazy." I thought if he were in that much pain, why wouldn't he just get up? Before I could finish bashing the insanity of the dog, I thought about myself. I was a lot like that old dog. I would go through many of my daily activities in very much the same pain. I had become burnt out of the work I was doing and the life I was living. Some days it was painful getting out of the bed to go do what I was tired and burnt out of doing. I would get up and force myself to go because I thought that was what I had to do. I was allowing the comfort of familiarity to hold me hostage.

I was doing a lot of moaning and groaning about my situation, but I was continuing to lie on my nail in pain instead of doing something about it. I was going to church and hearing powerful sermons about individuals who moved in their purpose. I listened to tapes, read books and watched programs about others' triumphs and victories, but I continued to remain on my nail.

One day, I was thinking about my future and where I was in life. I thought about the missed opportunities because of my decision to live in a comfortable pain. The pain of not doing what God purposed to do was aggravating and frustrating. I finally made a decision that I was going to move in a different direction. I knew that if I continued to live in this misery I would miss my opportunity.

I decided I was going to move forward even if I did not know how things would turn out. I knew life had to be better than the pain of frustration and discouragement I was dealing with. I made a decision to totally trust God at His Word and leave the rest up to Him. I developed a vision plan, implemented a strategy and went to work.

The desire to remain in your comfort zone is natural and, because of that instinctive need, we jump on the someday bandwagon and push our goals and dreams to the side until another day. Unfortunately, nothing ever happens. Tomorrow becomes next week, which soon leads to next year. Then next year leads to five years, then ten years. Eventually, the life you desired to live becomes a distant memory. You can't afford to fall into the trap of "someday" because it may never come.

If you are at a point in life that you are tired of moaning and groaning about your comfortable pain, now is the time to take hold of your life. You cannot spend another day tolerating a pain that you do not have to put up with. If you remain fearful of leaving your comfortable pain, your situations will remain the same ten days, ten months or ten years from now.

You have the power to choose to go in a different direction. You have the power to move from your pain and into your promise. If you are in a negative situation that is causing you problems and pain, maybe it is time take a fresh look at yourself; discover who you are, define where you want to be, develop a clear plan of action and move forward.

"Move out of your comfort zone. You can only grow if you are willing to feel awkward and uncomfortable when you try something new."
—Brian Tracy

CHAPTER 42

THE WORLD IS WAITING FOR YOUR VISION

"Now unto Him who is able to do exceeding, abundantly and above
all that we ask or think, according to the power that
works within us."
—Ephesians 3:20

The world is waiting for you to make an impact with your vision. You cannot wait for the perfect timing, the right situation or the right economic climate. You must start pursuing your vision now.

It is up to you if you are going to live the life God designed for you or not. God has done all He is going to do; now the rest is up to you. He is expecting you to make your move. He is waiting for you to step up to the plate.

You don't have to go to another seminar or workshop, watch another program or listen to another vision sermon to move your vision forward. It is time to do what you know to do. Every day you do not implement your vision is another day you, others and the world misses your contribution.

I admit I made too many excuses to "why" I could not live my vision. I would say, "I was too busy, someone was already doing what I wanted to do, I did not have enough education or my resources were too limited".

I crippled myself from moving forward in my vision because I simply spent too much time making excuses. The excuses left me exhausted before I ever got started. It was not until I made a conscious decision to stop wasting time making excuses and participate in the process of living my vision that my life began to turn in a different direction.

I remember reading motivational speaker and author Willie Jolley's book, It Only Takes a Minute to Change Your Life. In it, he wrote about the importance of time and how we should use our time more effectively. It really encouraged me to look at how I was using my time. Here is what he said:

"Friends time waits for no one. It moves on and keeps moving on. It does not stop for anything or anybody. It doesn't matter how much money you have, how much power you have, or how much prestige you have – time keeps moving on; therefore you have got to respect time and use it wisely because time doesn't care who you are. Time is the great equalizer. From its standpoint, everybody is equal. It gives the same dividend to the rich as to the poor, to the powerful as to the weak, to the big as to the small. Everybody has the same amount of time twenty-four hours per day not one minute more."

Whatever God is calling you to, I admonish you to walk in it. Do not let anyone, including your family, the enemy, others or even you, talk yourself out of your promise. You do not know what God will do with the book you write, the job you apply for, the business you start or the person you share the Gospel with.

If you do things God's way and not the world's way, you could be walking into a top-selling book, a multi-million dollar business or sharing the Gospel that changes someone's eternal destiny.

You do not know what God can do through you until you do what He designed you to do. I am not promising that you'll be a millionaire, that everyone will love you or that everything will happen the way you want, but I know when you realize your purpose from God, your life will never be the same.

Colors will become brighter, words will become more powerful, time will not be wasted, your energy will rise and your vision will become clearer. Start living your vision today because the world is waiting for what's in you.

Here is a brief list of things I suggest trying that will empower you to vision success. I have tried several and they have affected my life in a phenomenal way and there are several more I am implementing.

The list will challenge your old way of thinking, interfere with your comfort zone and change your normal routine. I admonish you to try some of them and see what happens.

1. Narrow your T.V. time to one hour or less a day.

2. Give up a half hour of sleep to work on your vision.

3. Spend thirty minutes or less on Facebook or searching on the internet unless you are working on your vision.

4. Spend at least thirty minutes a day in prayer.

5. Use the time you spend in the car for listening to the Word of God, inspirational / motivational books or empowering messages.

6. Take your lunch to work and go to a quiet place to meditate, read, pray or write. Places you can go to are the library, park or a quiet restaurant.

7. Spend no more than ten or fifteen minutes a day texting or talking on the phone.

8. Stop trying to do and be everything for everybody.

9. If you have children, you may want to narrow them down to participating in no more than two major activities.

10. When you are at your children's practices or rehearsals, work on your vision.

11. Use vacation time or personal days to take a mini vacation to work on you.

12. Exercise and eat right so you will have energy to do what you need to do.

13. Take a thirty-minute walk four or five days a week to pray, exercise and meditate.

14. Set aside time daily to read your written vision and goals.

15. Use a sixty-day prayer journal to write your prayers and the answers to those prayers.

16. Read and study your Bible thirty minutes or more a day to learn what God has to say.

17. Pray as a family nightly.

18. Take up a new hobby.

19. Start that business you have been talking and dreaming about.

20. Meet some new people or go to some different places to broaden your horizons.

21. Learn a new subject matter to expand your knowledge base and break up any mental monotony.

"... I refuse to rummage through my trash heap of failures. I will admit them. I will correct them. I will press on victoriously. No failure is fatal. It's OK to stumble...I will get up. It's OK to fail...I will rise again. Today I will make a difference."
—Max Lucado

THE BEGINNING

It is my goal that the principles contained in Vision Impact! encouraged, equipped and empowered you to live your God-designed vision with excellence. Each one of the forty-two messages was designed to provide you with the knowledge and understanding of the importance of having a vision from God, and to give you sound, practical instruction and effective tools necessary to bring your vision into reality. I pray that you were ignited from within with a passion to pursue your vision without wavering.

You were born with a vision to achieve something of significance that will impact your world. You have everything within you to live an extraordinary life. If you walk in your vision, you will be inspired and empowered to overcome the obstacles and barriers that will challenge it. Your vision will motivate you to live to your maximum potential so that it impacts the lives of even those who have not been born. May you see farther than your physical eyes can see and live the incredible vision God designed for your life.

"A vision from God will raise a passion and hunger within you to achieve the extraordinary. It will expand your thinking, increase your sight and elevate your walk. Get ready to take hold of your vision and impact your world."
— Bernard Haynes

www.ingramcontent.com/pod-product-compliance
Lightning Source LLC
Chambersburg PA
CBHW072007090426
42740CB00011B/2128